TRADING STRATEGIES 101

Discover the Psychology of a successful Trader, How to Use Simple Trading and Tools to Thrive in Bull, Bear, and Sideways Markets

BY BRIAN HALE

Contents

INTRODUCTION

"The goal of a successful trader is to make the best trades.
Money is secondary."
— Alexander Elder

You have probably learned that financial freedom requires taking ownership of your finances. Having a dependable cash flow allows you to live the life you want and not worry about how you will pay your bills or sudden expenses. Also, you aren't burdened with a pile of debt.

So, you sit and outline your money goals, including opportunities to bump your income without getting another job. You also imagine what it would be like to have as much money as you could ever want. Fortunately, the stock market provides this type of opportunity to you.

Yes, you cannot go wrong trading and investing in stocks. According to a 2022 stock market report by DayTradingz, between 53% and 58% of Americans engage in the stock market. Moreover, the wealthiest 10% of Americans own ten times as many stocks as other investors. Getting involved in the stock market can generate income immediately, serve as a vehicle to build wealth, and help you attain financial independence.

In fact, ask any financial expert, and you will hear historically that stocks are one of the keys to growing your money and building long-term wealth. However, while stocks can expand in value enormously over time, it is impossible to anticipate their day-to-day movement with 100% precision.

Perhaps, you have already thought about putting your money in the stock market, but then, you're afraid of how "risky" everyone says it is. Or maybe you started trading stocks already, but you aren't just getting your desired result. So, you start asking yourself questions like…

How can I earn a consistent income from the stock market?

What stocks do I trade that will yield the best return for me?

How do I access winning strategies that will make me money, whether in the bull, bear, or stock market?

Or perhaps, what's the holy-grail strategy famous investors like Benjamin Graham and Warren Buffett use to generate million-dollar returns?

If you've repeatedly asked yourself these questions, I want you to know that you aren't alone. The truth is that several people, including me, have asked similar questions, too, as we've experienced different challenges with making money from the stock market.

In fact, while a recent Gallup poll showed that nearly 6 in 10 American adults have money in the stock market, unless you've previously worked as an investment banker, you might have better odds of making money at the casino than with stocks.

Regardless of the questions you ask or the issues you face, everything can change if you read this book to the end. You will discover winning trading techniques you can easily use to make money in the stock market. What's more, these strategies will work even when everyone else is losing.

You're probably wondering who I am or why I am qualified to teach you about the stock market. My name is Brian Hale, and I started with less than $7000 in the stock market, and now, I have over a million dollars at work in my stock trading and investment accounts. By the time you read this, there is a good chance that number will be even bigger.

Stocks go up and down every day, and people make daily profits. However, most investors do not get the results they want from the stock market. Instead, they miss opportunities in the market. Or they may buy a stock only to see it go down when good news comes out for what seems to be no reason at all. Most people find the stock market to be very confusing and illogical.

In fact, researchers from the University of California found that 90% of retail investors and day traders lose money, which is why most people think winning in the stock market is simply a game of chance.

The problem, however, is that most first-time traders and investors aren't given the knowledge and information they need to make winning trades. Instead, "trading educators" and other so-called financial gurus spread bad advice that ultimately causes most traders and investors to lose money in the stock market.

As a result, these people experience frustration and confusion. They start to think that stock trading is all about luck or is a game rigged against them. But there is a method to the stock market madness. There are reasons why stocks move the way they do, and all you need to do to make money is to understand them.

Individual stocks appear to move illogically because everything you think you know about the stock market and investing is incorrect. Don't be sorry. If you've been paying attention to financial news over the years, you've probably noticed that most experts are also wrong at critical junctures in the financial markets. They, like everyone else, tend to become overly bullish at market tops and extremely bearish at market bottoms.

Now, this book you're reading right now changes everything.

Trading Strategies 101 will show you how trading and investing in stocks is tied to the idea of wealth building and financial freedom. Perhaps you got this book because you have at least a vague interest in stocks, but like so many others, you have no idea how to start. See this book as your financial market compass. It will help you understand the nitty-gritty of stock trading and how to leverage it to attain financial independence.

Once you understand the concepts in this book, you will begin to understand the ins and outs of the stock market. Then, you will trade stocks confidently instead of tying your stomach in knots, worrying about how the stock market will make your investments go up and down in value.

Don't be like most people who get average or worse results in the market because they don't believe in themselves. Such people just let their broker, who often knows less than they do, handle their money or park their money in a bunch of mutual funds and let things ride at the mercy of the market. They don't learn how to invest wisely for themselves.

You have to be flexible and use your brain to make money in stocks. Yes, it takes work, but success in the stock market means taking control of your money and separating yourself from the crowd.

Trading Strategies 101 can help you achieve just that as it reveals proven trading strategies and techniques, helping you learn the psychology of a trader. This book shows you how to navigate the stock market hype and find hidden gems worth your money. That way, you can move one step closer to claiming your financial independence.

In the end, you will be able to do the following:

- Understand the difference between trading and investing in stocks and why they're both essential for sustainable success in the market;

- The truth about how retail brokerages make money off everyday traders and how this can affect your returns;

- Why risk is a good thing—this will change how you think about trading;

- How to develop the mindset of a successful trader;

- Myths about the stock market that often result in wallet-burning losses;

- The most common reasons why beginner investors and traders lose money in stocks;

- Mistakes that rookies make when adding stocks to their watchlist, and what you can do to avoid bad picks;

- Simple candlestick patterns you can use to find trading opportunities no matter which way the market is moving;

- The three key technical indicators every first-time trader should be able to read—you'd be surprised how many miss these;

…and much more.

Trading Strategies 101 will help you understand how stocks move and how to manage your money so that you cut your losing stocks early and hold on to your winning stocks. That way, you'll become one of the top 10% of successful traders in the stock market who make almost all of the money.

Before you go any further, I want to warn you that Trading Strategies 101 will jolt you as it provides all the techniques I found helpful in trading stocks, whether in the bull, bear, or sideways market. It doesn't matter if you don't know how to read a stock chart or have never made an investment before. In the end, you will feel that making money through stock trading is a sure thing.

If you incorporate all the tips and guidance in this book, you'll soon develop the winning stock trader's mindset and experience an instant confidence boost in all your trading activities.

Meanwhile, as we proceed to the first chapter, I must advise you to prepare yourself because making a change requires deliberate effort. You'll have to take action and put in the work to get the result you want.

You can keep waiting for the "perfect time" to dip your toe in the market or take the guesswork out of trading and find out how to earn consistent returns with stocks; the choice is yours. But if you are ready to take that giant leap, I promise you will enjoy the process as it will be fun.

Are you feeling excited already?

Well, then, let's dive in!

Chapter 1:

Welcome to the World of Capital Markets

"It's not whether you're right or wrong that's important, but how much money you make when you're right and how much you lose when you're wrong."
— George Soros

First, what is the capital market?

Capital markets are financial institutions that provide for transactions of long-term financial products. These products include shares, bonds, debt instruments, debentures, ETFs, etc., made available by suppliers. Now, suppliers are institutions with capital to loan or invest, like banks and individual or company investors. They help people with viable business ideas yet little to no capital to become entrepreneurs and grow their businesses into big companies.

A capital market helps an economy by offering a platform to raise cash for business operations, development activities, or wealth accumulation. Generally, capital markets operate according to the circular flow of income model.

Capital markets include stock exchanges, equity markets, debt markets, options markets, etc. For example, companies require commercial operations funds and typically borrow from homes or individuals. Individual investors' or households' money is invested in these companies' shares or bonds on the capital market. Then, investors receive earnings as well as goods and services in exchange.

Throughout this book, our focus will be on the stock market. So in this chapter, we will look into the stock market, how it works, the different types of stock market movement, where to trade stocks, and how stock prices are determined.

How the Stock Market Works

You must have heard that stocks can be an excellent way to create wealth over time. Well, that's true. But then how much knowledge do you possess to build wealth with stocks?

The stock market is like an auction house and a shopping mall combined, comprising as many vendors as possible, including institutional and individual investors buying and selling various items, such as public companies listed on stock exchanges. In essence, the stock market is a collection of markets where stocks (pieces of ownership in businesses) are traded between investors.

The stock market acts as a primary and secondary market to display a company's stock. Generally, capital markets allow businesses to raise money by selling stocks to investors. So, the stock market allows companies to sell shares directly to investors through initial public offerings (IPO) to raise more money to expand their businesses. Companies can also complete multiple secondary offerings of stock when they need to raise extra funds, so long as investors are willing to buy. And since the stock market also allows investors to buy and sell stocks, it can result in profits or losses.

We also have professional traders who work in large institutions like investment banks or hedge funds. They buy and sell stocks using information and tools that aren't available to the general public.

Then, there are retail traders who trade stocks themselves. They simply buy stocks through online brokerages to earn profit for the short-term and then sell them off. Retail traders have access to the same information and tools as professional traders but aren't as skilled or experienced.

Buyers need specific information when purchasing stocks, and the sources of this information concerning buying and selling stocks will depend on your time horizon. It is also worth noting that government agencies like the Securities and Exchange Commission (SEC) regulate the stock market.

To invest in stocks for long-term capital accumulation, long-term income, or a combination of the two, it is crucial to thoroughly consider specific fundamentals and sources where more work is put in. Luckily, we will cover these factors in subsequent chapters.

How Stock Markets Move

Stock prices change daily due to market forces, like the force of demand and supply. For instance, if people who want to buy a stock surpass those who wish to sell, then the stock's price will increase. Likewise, if more people are interested in selling a stock than buying it, there would be more supply of the stock, and its price would crash.

1. **Bull markets**

A bull market occurs when stock prices rise, and investors are optimistic about the future. It is a condition in a financial market whereby a large portion of security prices are expected to rise or already rising. It is also a sustained period that usually lasts months or sometimes years.

Bull markets generally occur when a perceived economy is strengthening or already strong. They usually happen in line with fundamental factors like solid gross domestic product (GDP) and a drop in the unemployment rate. They often overlap with a rise in corporate profits.

2. **Bear markets**

A bear market is another financial market condition in which an enormous portion of security prices experiences prolonged price declines. It is when stock prices fall, and investors are pessimistic about the future. Bear markets mainly describe cases when market prices fall by 20% or more from a recently attained high position.

3. **Sideways markets**

A sideways market is one where an asset does not exhibit considerable bull or bear price movement but trades within its present price range. In other words, stock prices are neither rising nor falling—they are simply stable. A sideways market is also known as a ranging market.

Various factors determine the length of a sideways market, including current sentiment and news developments that may affect prices. However, sideways markets generally last only a few weeks. So if you intend to trade in such a market, it is best to do it in the short-term.

Based on stock charts and indicators, you can usually figure out which way the market is moving. And if any of these market types confuse you, do not worry; we will discuss them in detail in later chapters. But for now, just think of them as voting machines for each company. This means that the higher a company's stock price, the more people will vote in favor of the company. Likewise, the lower the price, the less confidence people will have in that company.

What You're Actually Buying

Stock, also known as equity, describes *any* company's ownership certificates, while shares are a particular company's stock certificate. Simply put, a stock is a piece of ownership in a company.

Purchasing shares owned by a company makes you a shareholder in the company; basically, you're buying a small part of the company. When you become a shareholder in a company, you're entitled to a portion of the company's profits and losses. You're also entitled to vote on certain company decisions (although this isn't always the case).

Stocks are traded on exchanges, which are like markets where buyers and sellers meet to buy and sell stocks. The New York Stock Exchange (NYSE) is the most famous stock exchange, but there are also exchanges in London, Tokyo, and Hong Kong. These exchanges are where traders and investors trade companies' shares as stocks.

How Stock Prices Are Determined

Generally, the stock market price is determined by supply and demand, just like any other market. When a stock is put up for sale in the market and sold, the buyer and seller exchange money for share ownership. The selling price of the stock now becomes the new market price. Then, when a second share is sold, this price becomes the latest market price, and so on.

A price is assigned when a company releases its shares for the first time. This initial public offering (IPO) serves as an assignment of value that ideally reflects the company's value. After that first offering, the stock starts to trade on secondary markets, the stock exchange. Then, the stock price will begin to go up and down depending on several factors, including economic changes, political events, industrial implementations (like policies), war, and environmental changes.

For highly traded stocks, there are ever-ready buyers and sellers constantly bidding and asking for new prices. This means that stock prices depend on what buyers and sellers are willing to pay. For instance, if someone is willing to pay $10 for a stock, but the seller only wants $5, the price will be $5. It is also important to note that a stock's price only indicates what people are willing to pay for it at a particular moment. And this is what makes it so hard to be a profitable trader.

Institutions trying to build enormous positions and brokerage firms working for individual investors will also bid for stocks. There will be a price upshoot if there are more buyers than sellers. But the stock price will plummet if there are more sellers than buyers.

Now, while we have established that stock prices are determined in the marketplace, where buyers and sellers meet, have you ever wondered what forces drive the stock market and affect a stock's price? Unfortunately, no mathematical equation can determine how a stock's price behaves. However, certain factors have some percentage influence, including fundamental factors, technical factors, market sentiment, etc.

Having studied and learned about the capital market, with an intense focus on the stock market, it is time we took our learning to the next step. In the next chapter, you will learn the difference between trading, investing, and gambling.

Key Takeaways

- The stock market is like an auction house and shopping mall combined, where stocks (pieces of ownership in businesses) are traded between investors.

- Capital markets allow businesses to raise money by selling stocks to investors.

- The stock market allows investors to buy and sell stocks, which can result in profits or losses.

- A bull market arises when stock prices go up, a bear market occurs when stock prices decline for a sustained period, and a sideways market results when stock prices are stable.

Chapter 2:
Gambling Vs. Trading

"Risk comes from not knowing what you're doing."
— Warren Buffett

Did you know that only about 5% of gamblers make money in the long run?

That's right!

On the other hand, trading can produce consistent profits with a solid trading plan and risk management strategy.

Although people often equate trading with gambling, that is an unfair comparison. Indeed, both pursuits are vastly different, but one thing they have in common is that they involve some risk.

However, when you understand what makes trading distinct from gambling, you will better understand what it truly takes to become successful.

Luckily, this chapter will examine the differences and similarities between trading and gambling. We will also discuss why trading is an excellent way to make money in the stock market, the basics of risk and reward, and how to create a trading plan.

Gambling Vs. Trading

Many tend to approach trading like they are gambling on a stock in the stock market; that is, they see it as a losing proposition. Perhaps, this is because gambling is much more accessible than trading or because only a few stock traders truly understand how trading works.

Traders despise high levels of risk and uncertainty, whereas gamblers thrive on it. So, to be a successful trader, you must first learn about the stock market, analyze the chart, use technical indicators, read financial statements, and then develop a trading plan.

Trading is about risk and reward, as risk is always involved, but if you manage your risk properly, you can still come out ahead. Your goal as a trader is to make the right predictions. Unfortunately, gambling is not a game for precise predictions; rather, it's all about the thrill. For instance, there is no way to know the odds of winning or losing when gambling. However, most traders hate this and thus try to avoid it.

With trading, it is more realistic to build long-term wealth by using a sound investment strategy and harnessing the power of mathematical models and basic analysis to calculate the odds of success. This is not something you can do with gambling. In other words, trading means more than relying on pure luck.

It's unwise to bank on future winnings to pay your bills because you cannot predict how much money you can make weekly or monthly. This is why gambling should be regarded solely as a recreational activity.

Furthermore, gambling is based primarily on chance. It takes advantage of a well-known psychological obsession in humans whereby we are willing to sacrifice something while expecting a more valuable return in the future. Someone must lose for someone to win at gambling. And all professional gambling is designed to ensure gambling companies don't lose. In other words, gambling is designed to stack the odds against you, and you will permanently lose money because you can't accurately tell the true odds of winning or losing.

Though there is always risk in trading, you can still succeed with a proper risk management strategy because there is no better tool than a sound and well-thought-out plan.

The Basics of Risk and Reward

Every trade has risks and rewards associated with it, and the amount of risk you are willing to take should align with your goals. For instance, if you are looking to make a quick profit, you will likely take on more risk, but if you want to build long-term wealth, you should focus on trades with less risk.

The key is to find a comfortable balance. Efficiently managing risk is essential for trading success, especially as it minimizes your losses while preserving the profits from your winning investments. Understanding a transaction's risk/reward ratio makes it easier to pick which setups to pursue and choose what would optimize your net profits.

As traders, we always look for strategies to achieve a higher payoff with less risk. Ideally, the better you limit your losses, the more you may increase your net gains from winning transactions. And the fact that a trader who wins just half of their trades might be lucrative emphasizes the necessity of risk management.

The objective is to keep your average loss smaller than your average profit; this is what we mean by having a better risk/reward ratio.

The risk/reward ratio measures how much profit you stand to make for every dollar you risk on a trade. It calculates the possible risk and reward for each trade, allowing you to objectively compare potential trades and fine-tune your entire trading strategy accordingly. In subsequent chapters, we will discuss this in more detail, including how to calculate your risk/reward ratio and other factors to consider.

In addition, to define your risk tolerance, which depends on how much you are trading, you also need to consider your psychological makeup. And this is because the most challenging aspect of trading is managing emotions. For instance, a successful trader may teach a novice their strategy. However, the beginner may ultimately lose all their money since they cannot keep their feelings aside, which is a fact in the trading business. Most novices can't cut their losses when the trading system tells them to exit; they also can't accept their wins either because they want to stay on for more significant profit.

So, are you the type of person who can handle taking a loss? Or do you tend to panic and sell when the market takes a dip? It is important to know yourself before you start trading.

How to Make Money as a Trader

In the simplest terms, you make money as a trader by buying low and selling high. Making money as a stock trader is based entirely on hypothesizing about the rise and fall of a company's stock prices. Traders place buy and sell orders that yield a profit if their trade thesis is correct and a loss if it is incorrect. The size of a stock trader's shares and the dollar equivalent of their shares determine how much money they make. Now, let's discuss the specific ways a trader can make money.

1. Buy low and sell high

Through this method, stock traders buy a stock when it's cheap and hold it until it appreciates; then, they sell it off at a higher price. For instance, let's say it's 2012, and you think Facebook could be worth much more in a couple of years than it is now. You may then buy $5,000 worth of Facebook shares at $40 per share, which amounts to 125 shares. One decade later, you return to your trade and find that Facebook's stock price is now $330 per share. Remember, you own 125 shares of Facebook, and at $330 per share, your initial $5,000 investment is now worth $41,250.

You bought Facebook when it was "low" and correctly predicted it would rise in value, making you sell it at a higher price. This is one of the simplest ways to buy low and sell high.

2. Short-selling

Short-selling is another way to make money with stocks. With this strategy, the goal is to sell high and buy low. For instance, let's assume it's 2007, and you're concerned about the housing crisis and how it might affect banks that own many widely traded mortgage-backed securities. Suddenly, you discover a stock you believe is vulnerable to the housing crisis. It is currently trading at around $120 per share, and you think it will continue to fall, so you decide to short-sell the stock. But how do you sell a stock you don't own?

Technically, you "borrow" the shares from someone who already owns them, sell them, and then repurchase them at a lower price, pocketing the difference. Eventually, the stock fell from $120 per share to $60 per share over the next several months. But because you were pretty foresighted and correctly predicted that the shares would drop, you closed it out for a $60 per share profit.

3. Dividends

Buying dividend stocks is another innovative way for a stock trader to make money. Dividend stocks are stocks that pay income to investors quarterly or annually through a dividend, which is a small cash allocation from an organization to its shareholders as a reward for purchasing their stock. A shareholder's dividend is frequently a percentage of their investment.

As a result, whenever the company pays a dividend, you can deposit the dividend proceeds into your account or funnel them into more shares, increasing the size of your position.

There are endless ways to make money from trading, but the key is to have a plan. Your trading plan should consider what stock you want to trade, when you want to trade, and how much risk you are willing to take. It is also important to have an exit strategy before entering a trade. This way, you know when to cut your losses, take your profits, and move on.

While people think you can earn huge profits off single trades, you need to gradually build up to that level with incremental gains. And much of those gains start with your skill base and knowledge as a trader.

Key Takeaways

- Gambling and trading are not the same. Trading is a more systematic way to make money in the stock market.

- Risk and reward are key concepts in trading. Every trade has an associated amount of risk and reward, so it is important to find a comfortable balance.

- You can make money as a trader by buying low and selling high. And although there are endless ways to profit from trading, the key is to have a plan.

Chapter 3:
Trading Vs. Investing

"It is not the strongest . . . that survive, nor the most intelligent, but the one most responsive to change."
— Charles Darwin

When discussing making money in the stock market, it is important to get the basics right because many people think that trading and investing are the same. However, there are significant differences between the two.

For instance, investors seek higher returns over time by purchasing and holding stocks. However, traders leverage rising and falling markets to enter and exit positions in a shorter time frame, taking smaller and more frequent profits. In essence, trading and investing both involve seeking profit in the stock market, but they pursue that goal differently. Fortunately, we will cover the differences between trading and investing and why trading is a more active and faster way to make money in the stock market.

What Exactly Is Trading?

Trading is an active, short-term strategy for making money in the stock market since it involves frequent transactions depending on market trends. It is a faster way to earn compared to long-term transactions such as mutual funds or bonds. Trading simply involves buying and selling stocks quickly, usually based on technical analysis or a gut feeling.

There are three types of stock trading:

- **Active trading:** This is when an investor makes ten or more trades each month. Also, they frequently employ techniques that rely largely on market timing. Then, they try to profit from short-term occurrences (at the company or in the market) by capitalizing on them.

- **Day trading:** This refers to buying and selling a stock on the same day. Day traders are uninterested in the inner workings of firms. Instead, they try to profit from daily price movements within minutes and hours.

- **Scalp trading:** This involves traders buying and holding positions for a few seconds or minutes rather than overnight.

Overall, the goal of trading is to make small, consistent profits over time. For instance, if a long-term investor gets 10–15% of profit annually, a trader can earn the same amount monthly based on their choices and actions.

But that's not all; trading is dynamic and volatile. Therefore, as a trader, you need to be able to handle risk and be comfortable with taking losses and not just profits.

What Is Investing?

Investing is a long-term strategy focusing on buying and holding onto stocks for a period. Unlike trading, the goal of investing is to make a large profit from the appreciation in the stock price over time. This means investors are more averse to risk and often seek to preserve their capital.

Investments are usually held for years, if not decades, to reap rewards such as interest, dividends, and stock splits. While markets will inevitably fluctuate, investors will "ride out" downtrends, assuming that prices will increase and losses will be recovered. Fundamental market indicators, such as price-to-earnings ratios and management forecasts, are usually more important to investors.

Investing relies less on technical and fundamental analysis, such as a company's marketing and financials. The investment appreciates when a corporation develops a hot, new product that improves sales, increases revenues, and raises the stock's market value.

Anyone who owns a 401(k) or an IRA is investing, even if they are not constantly monitoring their investment's performance. And because the goal is to develop a retirement account over time, various mutual funds' day-to-day volatility is less essential than continuous growth over time.

When you buy a stock, you expect the firm to develop and perform well over time. When this occurs, your shares may become more valuable, and other investors may be ready to purchase them for a higher price than you paid. So if you choose to sell them, you could make a profit. Investing is a tried-and-true method of putting your money to work for you while you work to earn more of it in other ways.

The Difference between Trading and Investing

As you can see, both trading and investing seek profit in the stock market, but they do so differently. However, their main difference is that trading is more active and has a shorter time horizon, while investment is more passive and has a longer time horizon. This makes trading riskier than investing, especially as traders need to use leverage to buy and hold more positions.

While traders move equities in and out in weeks, days, or even minutes in pursuit of short-term profits, investors have a long-term perspective. Investors generally keep equities despite market turbulence because they think in terms of years. Scalpers may only be in a position for a few minutes. Likewise, day traders are just concerned with the trading day, whereas swing traders invest for several days or weeks.

Traders and investors also have different goals. For instance, traders usually concentrate on a stock's technical characteristics rather than a company's long-term potential. They are also interested in which direction the stock will go next and how they might profit from that move. However, investing relies more on fundamental analysis, which we will cover in Chapter 10.

Investors examine a company's potential for long-term development or value before buying and holding a stock. However, traders usually profit from minor market mispricing, such as when political turmoil in a foreign country momentarily drives down the share price of a U.S. manufacturer.

How Trading and Investing Work Together

At their most basic level, trading and investing are identical. For instance, they involve opening an account to buy and sell investments. They also offer the chance to pick from a wide range of investment types to help you reach your personal goals. These similarities make them integrate well with each other. In this section, we will explore how trading and investing work together.

You see, trading can be a great way to generate income to reinvest in investments, especially if you're good at it. However, investing can provide the capital to trade with.

When you invest in the stock market, you create the opportunity for your investment's value to compound. And the power of compounding increases over time.

However, compounding may only sometimes work to your advantage, particularly with shorter deadlines. However, when stock prices fall, your losses will compound. Then, you must recover a bigger percentage of what you lost to compensate for the losses. For example, if a $100 investment drops by 10% to $90, it will require more than a 10% gain to return to the initial $100.

While compounding's benefits and drawbacks affect both investors and traders, trading may be riskier when it comes to compounding due to the shorter time frame to recover losses. However, investing for the long-term allows your money to recover and flourish after a slump.

In addition, trading is a good way to diversify your portfolio and reduce your reliance on the stock market. The two strategies can also be used to hedge each other's risks. For example, if, as an investor, you are worried about a stock market crash, you can use trading to short-sell the market, protect your portfolio, and even make a profit.

On the other hand, investing is a good way to grow your wealth in the long-term. It is a more passive strategy requiring less time and energy than trading. It is also less risky than trading, making it a good option for risk-averse people. Trading should normally represent a percentage of your total investments, not your entire portfolio, due to the high degree of risk involved. This allows you to place riskier investments without endangering long-term financial prospects.

As we wrap up, one tip we usually come across is to trade or invest in stocks. But the reality is that making such a move can be intimidating for many people, especially due to the several misconceptions we hear and read about the capital market daily. But to make things easier for you, we will bust some common myths you might have heard about trading and investing in the next chapter.

Key Takeaways

- Trading is an active, faster way to make money in the stock market while investing is a more passive and slower money-making strategy.

- Trading involves more risk than investing and relies more on technical analysis.

- The goals of trading and investing are different. For instance, traders aim to make small, consistent profits over time, while investors seek to make a large profit from the appreciation in stock price over time.

- Despite their differences, trading and investing can work well together.

Chapter 4:
Fact or Fiction—Myths of the Financial Market

"The goal of a successful trader is to make the best trades. Money is secondary."
— Alexander Elder

You've probably heard many claims about the stock market, such as "You have to time the market perfectly to make money." It also seems everyone has an opinion on why you should or shouldn't trade and invest in the stock market, not to mention how to do it.

However, these claims are often false, especially those media headlines that are mere clickbait or doomsday predictions from social media friends or followers. In reality, the stock market is much more complex, and many factors will determine your success as a trader.

So, don't let stock market myths stop you from investing. This chapter dispels common misconceptions about the stock market to enable you to distinguish fact from myth so you can trade and invest confidently. You will also learn the importance of having a long-term perspective when trading.

Myth #1: You Need to be an Expert to be Successful

The prevalent stock trading idea that one needs to be an expert—perhaps in finance or economics—to be a successful trader is a myth. Stock trading is becoming increasingly accessible.

Sure, it helps if you have some knowledge about the stock market and how it works. However, you don't need a degree to attain the relevant knowledge for trading stocks.

Plenty of successful traders and investors are not experts; the key is to educate yourself as much as possible and always do your own research before trading or investing. You could also hold regular meetings with other traders to share information.

Myth #2: You Need to Trade Often to be Successful

While it would be good to imagine that if a trader earns money once a day, they may make ten times as much trading ten times a day, this is rarely the case. Trading less and focusing on a few stocks you understand will benefit you in the long run. You do not need to trade often to be successful in the stock market. In fact, many successful investors only make a handful of trades each year.

Unless a trader is talented and focuses on scalping tactics, most traders will gain by being patient, focusing on something they know, and waiting for the greatest opportunities, which may be few and far between. Ultimately, the key is to find good companies you believe in and then hold on to those stocks for the long-term.

Myth #3: You Need to Pick hot Stocks to be Successful

The appeal of hot stocks is understandable. Your neighbor, who drives a fancy car, mentions some hot stock he likes, and you're instantly hooked. Or maybe you find a list of hot stocks online featuring surging stocks. And if a stock is up by 10% today or has doubled over the past year, it must have some merit, right? I mean, who wouldn't want to double their money in a single year?

But while it's true that you can make a lot of money by investing in hot stocks, it is also very risky. Hot stocks are problematic because they are over-valued and will eventually come crashing down, taking your hard-earned money with them. So you would often do better investing in less exciting stocks.

Myth #4: You Need to Time the Market Perfectly to be Successful

Despite what many veteran investors or stock traders on social media may tell you, nobody knows what the market will do. Timing the market is incredibly difficult, as you have to decide when to exit the market and when to buy back in. Even the most experienced investors struggle to correctly time the market.

The stock market fluctuates based on investor confidence, economic data, political uncertainty, and more, making it extremely difficult to time the market. However, timing the market is unnecessary.

Instead of trying to time the market, the best route for long-term investing success is to stay the course. So, avoid getting wrapped up in the day-to-day news cycle and let your initial investment strategy play out instead. It is better to buy stocks when they are undervalued and then hold on to them until they reach their full potential.

Remember those 10- and 30-year average returns from earlier? They ranged from 8% to 12%. So you do not need to pick a day when the market drops to start investing; ultimately, the goal is to invest with long-term returns.

Myth #5: The Stock Market Is Random

Statisticians term the volatile movements of the stock market as a "random walk" (like staggering drunkenly on the sidewalk). However, the truth is the stock market often exhibits a steady rather than random trend.

The valuation of a stock reflects the relative strength of the underlying business. Furthermore, underlying fundamentals, such as company earnings, economic indicators, and global events, drive a stock's valuation.

If a business implements innovative changes, revenue may rise and increase the valuation of the company's stock. And while some element of luck and speculation is involved, the stock market is not a gambling game.

Myth #6: The Biggest Companies Are the Safest Investments

Don't let size and numbers deceive you—many of these big companies you know are not as stable as they look. And the reasons are numerous, as the business world and its problems are now more complex than ever.

In fact, some of the world's biggest companies have filed for bankruptcy, including General Motors, Lehman Brothers, and Enron. Others have substantially reduced in size and fallen from an industry leadership position. So, do not blindly invest in a company because it is large and well-known.

The world has changed dramatically since many well-known and trusted "rocks" of business were born. However, reinvention, improvement, and the ability to disrupt the market are required at a faster rate than many companies can keep up with. Therefore, you should do your research to find out if a company is truly a good investment before investing in it.

Myth#7: You Can Get Rich with a Few Trades

You've probably seen adverts where people talk about the joys of stock trading while standing in front of a Ferrari with a bundle of cash and telling stories of how they became billionaires overnight. However, these adverts are, at best, deceptive. At worst, they indicate the presence of a con artist at work.

Stock trading is not a get-rich-quick scheme, so don't expect to get rich with just a few trades. Many novice investors try to make money fast with stock trading and lose all of their money.

Stock trading and investing necessitates research and effort. They can provide a stable income for people prepared to put in the time to learn about the market. And since the stock market is the world's greatest market, there is profit to be made.

However, don't expect to make much money in your first year. It is important to remember that the stock market is a long-term game. To succeed, you need patience and discipline, especially when starting.

Myth #8: Buying and Holding Stocks Forever Is the Best Way to Go

You have probably heard that jumping in and out of stocks leads to losses, so buying and holding stocks for the long-term is better.

However, a leading stock's average run lasts 12–18 months before falling into a strong and sustained drop. Worse yet, once a major stock reaches its peak, it sometimes never returns. But if it does, it usually takes many years.

So, what happens when the stock's bull run ends? Well, it either stops rising or falls, taking your earnings with it. Meanwhile, other equities rise unless the market is in a bear market. So, it is better to realize when a stock's run has ended, sell it, and invest the proceeds in a stock showing signs of growth. That way, you won't be sitting on dead money or, worse, losses.

The key point in this chapter is that trading and investing in the capital market is systematic. Successful stock traders and investors use strategic approaches when buying stocks, which is exactly what you should be doing.

So, reorientate your mind about these misconceptions and start working on approaching the stock market in a way that would benefit you. And to further help you set the right foundation for your trading journey, we will look at why so many people lose money in the stock market in the next chapter.

Key Takeaways

- Many people believe many myths and misconceptions about the stock market.

- You do not need to be an expert or trade often to be successful.

- Picking hot stocks is risky, and timing the market is difficult.

- The stock market is not random but driven by fundamentals.

Chapter 5:
Why Most Traders and Investors Lose

"Amateurs think about how much money they can make. Professionals think about how much money they could lose."
— Jack Schwager

Did you know that over 90% of traders and investors lose money in the stock market? That's right!

When new traders and investors get started in the stock market, they are often disappointed when the stock value drops below their purchase price. Not understanding the drop in purchase value, often leads to traders and investors making impulsive decisions that make them lose money.

It's common to experience this in your trading and investing adventures; I know because several others and I did. But while stock traders can lose money in different ways, they mostly lose money for a select few reasons. And although most of these reasons may seem obvious, they're easy to ignore or forget, especially if you are new to the trading and investing game.

This chapter will explore why people lose money in the stock market. We will also discuss the most common mistakes traders and investors make, such as not having a plan, overtrading, not managing risk, and many more. In the end, you will understand the importance of having realistic expectations and staying disciplined.

Not Planning Ahead

This is one major mistake people make when they start trading and investing in the stock market. They fail to create a plan to guide their trading decisions. Instead, they easily trust tips and recommendations from a friend, colleague, brokerage firm, or financial advisor. Sadly, these recommendations often result in a major loss on their investment.

Remember, no one else cares about your money more than you do. Therefore, you must have a good investment plan that covers your investment goals, risk tolerance, and time horizon. That way, you won't be tempted to make impulsive trading and investing decisions that can lead to losses.

You are too Overconfident

This happens a lot in the financial market. Usually, a random person accumulates so much profit through trading or investing in the stock market over a specific period. Then, one day, they are thinking of how they have increased their capital and imagine that by doubling their risk exposure per trade, they should be able to make even more money. After all, if they can earn so much money in the stock market, why can't they make even more in a shorter period?

As a result, they enter the stock market with a large sum of money saved over many years of hard work. But this is where they fall short.

Many believe they know more about the markets than they do, leading them to make poor investment decisions. It is important to remember that even the most experienced investors and traders can make mistakes.

You Fail to Diversify

As you gain experience as an investor, you realize that diversifying your assets is critical to success. Even as a beginner, you'll always read about diversification.

Diversification is important because it helps to reduce risk. Failure to diversify your portfolio could expose you to bigger risks in case of stock market corrections, rough economies, or a company crashing.

For example, certain stock funds might have a higher reward but high risk. So, if you went all in, you could do well in a good market.

However, once the market starts declining, you could lose all returns and potentially more.

By investing in various asset classes, you can protect yourself from losses if one particular asset class declines in value. A diverse portfolio includes several industries and categories that react differently from one another. Ultimately, this reduces trade and investment risks.

You are only Chasing Performance

It can be tempting to try to capitalize on the gains when an asset class or individual security has had a strong run-up in price. Sadly, so many rookie traders and investors make this mistake. They chase performance, which often leads to buying assets at inflated prices and can eventually lead to losses when the market corrects.

Most hot stocks and industries usually belong to this list. And this is because when everyone starts talking about some specific names, more investors believe they should own it, giving it more traction. But you can't tell when the strong run-up will end, which could leave you at a loss if you bought the stock at its peak price.

Therefore, I recommend you not go with the herd if you want to profit from the stock market. Instead, if you want to find profitable companies, look among the less popular small-cap and microcap firms, not the ones everyone is talking about. Make a solid investing strategy and stick to it.

You React Easily to News

It is important to remember that the markets are efficient, and prices reflect all available information. People frequently lose money in the markets because they are unfamiliar with economic and financial market cycles.

Business and economic cycles grow and contract. A growing economy, an increasing job market, and other economic reasons drive boom cycles. However, when inflation begins to rise, prices rise, and GDP growth slows. In this situation, the stock market's value may also fall.

However, there is no need to react to every piece of news that drops as the stock market rises and falls due to global events. Doing so will only lead to emotionally driven decisions that are not based on sound analysis.

For example, the Dow lost 7.1% on the first trade day after 9/11 (September 17, 2001). It was the largest one-day point loss in the index's history at the time. If you had sold during the week following 9/11, your investments would most likely have lost money. However, if you had stayed the course and done nothing after the decline, you would have been rewarded. The S&P 500, NASDAQ, and Dow Jones Industrial Average all returned to pre-attack levels within a month.

You Lack Patience

Although investing is a long-term game, and it takes time to achieve results, many people lack the patience to succeed. As a result, they make impulsive decisions that usually lead to losses. You shouldn't force a trade when the opportunity isn't there.

In addition, being impatient and changing trading strategies frequently is one of the biggest mistakes that day traders make.

Another mistake they make is rushing to book their profits or making trading decisions in a hurry, which is one of the reasons they incur losses. Worse yet, some traders even book profits before deciding their price targets or stop-loss. However, successful traders execute their trades in a planned way, like determining their stop-loss and profit target level and then only executing their trades.

You are not Learning From Your Mistakes

In today's fast-paced world, most of us find learning tough, especially when it's about trading and investing in the stock market. Many regular judgments lack objective feedback, and decision-making biases confuse our ostensibly rational thinking.

For example, if we see good prior returns on investment, were those profits earned by skill or luck?

Many individuals attribute excellent trades to talent and bad trades to chance—specifically, bad luck or forces beyond our control. Despite all these forces working against them when they make mistakes, they still fail to learn from those mistakes.

Everyone makes mistakes, but the most successful investors and traders learn from them and use them to improve their investment strategies.

You are not Managing Risk

All investments carry some risk, but not managing risk can lead to large losses that could have been easily avoided.

Using stop-losses and correctly sizing your position will save you from incurring huge losses from the stock market. A stop-loss order is a type of order through which traders can instruct a broker to sell the stocks below their purchasing price to reduce losses. As this order gets immediately executed, intraday traders can reduce the loss if the price movements go against their expectations. (We will discuss stop-loss orders in detail in Chapter 7.)

Unfortunately, some novice traders do not set stop-losses in their trades, resulting in huge losses. As a trader, you should aim to maximize your profits while also protecting your capital and preventing losses.

You Overindulge in Leverage

If leverage works in your favor, money-making can be magnified. But if it goes against you, it can put you on the verge of bankruptcy. Leverage can be beneficial when used well, but too much leverage can lead to large losses.

Overindulging in leverage has made many traders receive margin calls from their brokers, especially when a sudden surge in volatility results in stock prices going against them. And once such a cycle starts, troubles increase due to its viciousness. But in the end, the stock market is a good teacher. It teaches us to stay on the ground.

Therefore, it's important to use leverage cautiously and only when comfortable with the risks involved.

You do not Track Results

Trading can be an overwhelming arena; a lot is always happening in the market. For instance, market trends change, traders change strategies, currencies prices fall or rise, and so on.

Unless you keep track of everything that happens as you trade, holding yourself accountable for both your wins and losses is nearly impossible. Moreover, it's also challenging to learn and improve your trading skills. If you don't track your investment results, it won't be easy to know what is working and what isn't.

Without tracking your results, you will be likelier to repeat mistakes and miss out on opportunities. So record all your trading activities in a trading journal and review them from time to time to track your results.

You Don't Understand Taxes

Whether you planned an investment strategy for months or a piece of stock news aroused your interest in the market, you may not have given your taxes any thought.

Trading and investing in stocks can be an excellent way to build money. However, just like your regular salary, the money you produce is taxable. Investors and traders need to know the tax implications of their investment activity.

Not understanding the taxes can lead to paying more in taxes than necessary or even incurring penalties.

You are too Busy Trying to Time the Market

Although we discussed this subject in the previous chapter, it's too important to avoid bringing it up again. Numerous research studies by disinterested parties have already demonstrated the failures of market timing.

It is impossible to predict short-term market movements consistently; attempting to do so will only lead to losses. That includes anticipating a drop and predicting when the market will recover. The decision to limit stock exposure by transferring assets to money market investments or cash entails anticipating when to leave and reenter the market.

You do not Review Your Strategy

Let's be real—a lot goes into each of your trades, like preparing, choosing the right stock, monitoring it, and reviewing it so you can improve. You'll already know about all this if you have been going through my *Investing for Beginners* series.

You must gain knowledge and practice your skills before starting to trade in the real markets. But once you start trading, does the fine-tuning process stop? Should you just trade on autopilot mode now?

Of course not! You still have to improve constantly, and that happens by reviewing your trades. Sadly, many traders and investors fail to review their strategies.

Regularly reviewing your investment strategy is important to ensure it is still working for you. Winning traders assess and evaluate their trading results regularly. They recognize that trading is a skill that can only be honed through consistent practice.

You let Your Emotions Take Over

Although being human and expressing your feelings can be beneficial, when your emotions take over, this can lead to costly blunders and poor investing decisions. It's difficult not to make emotional decisions in the face of the media, stock market volatility, others advising you on what to do, and your relationship with individual assets. Yet, it's a big reason people lose money in the stock market.

However, it's important to remain calm and disciplined when investing. And you can do so by sticking to your trading game plan and protecting yourself during rough stock market years.

As we wrap up this chapter, it's worth noting that your investments and strategy will alter as you get older. But for the time being, it's crucial to understand why most individuals lose money in the stock market. That way, you can avoid becoming part of that herd. And to further set you on the right path, we will examine the psychology behind the successful trader in the next chapter.

Key Takeaways

- Many people think they know more about investing than they do, which can lead to making poor decisions.

- Diversification is important to reducing risk.

- Chasing performance often leads to buying assets at inflated prices.

- Investing is a long-term game; it takes time to achieve results.

Chapter 6:
The Psychology of a Successful Trader

"Never, ever argue with your trading system."
– Michael Covel

Many people think that making money in the stock market is about being smart and knowing what to do. While these are important, there are other crucial factors to consider. For instance, psychology plays a big role in trading, and successful traders must have the right mindset.

Unfortunately, in education, there is a definite void in the market. There is hardly any material that addresses trading psychology at a deep enough level of insight to effectively help someone understand why success is so elusive.

And that is why I put this chapter together. It covers the importance of psychology in trading and how to develop the mindset of a successful trader. You will learn about important topics such as greed, fear, and confidence and how they can affect your trading decisions. We also discuss the importance of staying calm and focused when trading.

The Importance of Psychology in Trading

Stock traders and investors must compete not only with other stock traders but also with themselves. You are usually your worst enemy as a stock trader or investor. This is because we are naturally emotional beings. Our egos want to be validated—we want to prove to ourselves that we know what we're doing and that we can care for ourselves. We also have an innate survival instinct.

Now and then, all of these emotions and instincts can come together to reward us with trading wins. However, most of the time, our emotions get the best of us and cause us to lose money in the market unless we learn to control them.

Many stock traders believe it would be great to separate oneself from one's emotions. But, unfortunately, that is nearly impossible, especially since some emotions may help you succeed in trading. That is why understanding yourself as a trader is the best thing you can do for yourself.

Yes, psychology plays a big role in trading, and successful traders must have the right mindset. So, you need to identify your strengths and weaknesses and understand the key psychological factors that affect trading, such as greed, fear, and overconfidence.

1. **Greed**

On Wall Street, there's an ancient adage that says "pigs get butchered." This refers to greedy investors' practice of holding on to a winning position for too long to get every last tick higher in price. Eventually, the trend reverses, and the greedy are caught.

While greed is difficult to fight because it is often based on the impulse to do better and acquire a little more, a trader should learn to recognize this inclination and establish a trading plan based on logic rather than whims or feelings.

2. **Fear**

When traders receive negative news regarding a certain stock or the economy in general, they naturally become concerned. They may overreact and liquidate their assets to avoid the risk of severe losses. However, while they may avoid certain losses, they may also miss out on some rewards.

Traders must recognize fear as a natural response to a perceived threat; it threatens their earning potential, and quantifying the fear may be beneficial.

Successful traders evaluate their fears and why they are afraid of them. But they think about the fear before bad news occurs, not in the middle of it. By thinking ahead, they understand how they see and react to circumstances automatically and can transcend beyond their emotional responses.

Of course, this is not easy, but it is essential for the health of an investor's portfolio, not to mention the investor themselves.

3. **Overconfidence**

Overconfidence is an over-inflated belief in your stock trader and investor skills. If you think you have got everything figured out, have nothing more to learn, and money is yours for the stock market, you probably suffer from overconfidence.

Unfortunately, overconfident traders and investors tend to get into trouble by trading too frequently or placing extremely large trades as they go for the home run. I gave an example in the previous chapter. Inevitably, an overconfident trader will end up either trading in and out of trades—churning the trader's account—or risking too much on the one trade that goes bad and wipes out most of their account.

The best way to overcome overconfidence is to establish a strict set of risk-management rules. These rules should at least cover how many trades you will allow yourself to be in at a time, how much of your account you are willing to risk on each trade, and how much of your account you are willing to lose before you take a break from trading and re-evaluate your trading strategy.

By limiting the number of trades you are willing to be in and the amount of risk you are willing to take, you can spread your risk out evenly over your portfolio. We'll cover more on risk management in subsequent chapters.

Knowing these psychological factors and how they affect trading decisions is important. To succeed, you must stay calm and focused when trading or investing in the stock market.

Developing the Mindset of a Successful Trader

Aside from formulating better strategies and performing more extensive analysis, you must develop a winning mindset to succeed. Many studies of traders have revealed what distinguishes a winning trader from a failing one:

- It is not true that winning traders devise better trading techniques.

- It's not that winning traders are more intelligent.

- It's not that winning traders perform superior market analysis.

Rather, it's that the psychological perspective of a winning trader differs from that of a failing trader. Oh, yes! Developing the right mindset to be a successful trader and investor is important.

Psychologically, the very best traders share the same key characteristics. And if you want to become a successful trader, you need to develop these key qualities.

1. Investigate and be curious

As a trader or investor in the stock market, it's important to devote as much time as possible to the research process before making any investment decisions. You want to know what kind of firm you're investing in, so you should become an expert in the stocks and industries that interest you.

You should also stay up to date on the news, educate yourself, and, if feasible, attend trading seminars and conferences. This entails analyzing charts and the company's financial statements, consulting with the management, reading trade periodicals, and conducting additional background research such as macroeconomic analysis, industry analysis, and an evaluation of the overall market conditions. Doing these will give you the confidence you need to navigate risk.

2. Stay disciplined

Successful traders and investors are disciplined people who can observe the market objectively regardless of how current market action affects their account balance. They can respond swiftly to shifting market conditions and do not fall in love with and "marry" their market study.

If price activity suggests that they should adjust their outlook on likely future price fluctuations, they do so without hesitation.

And this is exactly what you want to be doing. You should stick to your investment plan and not let emotions influence your decisions. Because when you let your emotions take over, it can lead to impulsive and irrational decision-making, which can be costly.

You should put in the effort and take the necessary steps to become a self-disciplined trader who follows tight money and risk management guidelines. Winning traders are not irresponsible gamblers. Before taking each trade, they carefully weigh potential risk versus potential reward.

3. Be patient

When it comes to trading and investing in the stock market, you need to have a lot of patience. You need to be patient in both good and bad times. For instance, when the market is down, it can be tempting to sell all your stocks to avoid further losses. However, successful investors know that these downturns are temporary and that they provide opportunities to buy quality stocks at bargain prices.

Similarly, successful stock traders patiently wait for profits after buying a stock. Of course, just because you buy a stock does not mean you will immediately start making money on it. It may take months or even years to appreciate and generate profits.

4. Have realistic expectations

While making a lot of money in the stock market, it is also possible to lose lots of money. And that's because stock prices can go up and down.

Therefore, it is important only to invest money that you can afford to lose without putting your financial future at risk. Successful traders and investors don't become overly thrilled about winning trades or depressed about losing trades.

They control their emotions rather than letting their emotions control them.

As you can see, one key factor separating winning traders from losers is their psychological mindset. Successful traders can tame their greed, deal with fear, and avoid being overconfident in the market. They are also ready to accept risk and the fact that they may be wrong more often than they are right when making trading decisions. And that brings us to the next subject—**risk**, whose role in trading we will cover in the next chapter.

Key Takeaways

- Factors such as greed, fear, and overconfidence can affect trading decisions.

- It is important to stay calm and focused when trading.

- Developing the right mindset allows you to make money while everyone else is losing their minds over the markets.

Chapter 7:
Risky Business

"In investing, what is comfortable is rarely profitable."
— Robert Arnott

L et's face it—most people who go into trading and investing in stocks want to make money, but very few give thought to the risks involved.

Risk is everywhere! Our actions to improve our future may not work out or even work against us. However, as long as we are prepared to handle downs, our determination and patience carry us to the ups.

This philosophy applies to the stock market, too. Using capital to reach a profit potential, whether as a trader or an investor, comes with a risk of loss. Thus, to preserve our investments and avoid financial losses, we apply various risk management approaches.

Luckily, this chapter covers the importance of risk management, the different types of risk involved in trading, and how to manage them. We will cover vital topics such as stop-losses, position sizing, and risk-reward ratios.

Why You Must Create a Risk Management Plan

We apply risk management to minimize losses should the market tide turn against our trades after an unexpected event. Although the temptation to seize any opportunity exists for all traders, we must understand the hazards of a trade or an investment in advance to ensure we can withstand them if things go wrong.

Therefore, it's important to have a risk management plan before beginning to trade or invest in stocks. This plan should include an evaluation of your risk tolerance and the strategies you will use to manage risk.

You should also have a plan for what to do if your investments start to lose money. Without a plan, it's easy to make rash decisions that might cost you a lot of money.

All successful traders understand and recognize that trading is a complex process and that having a comprehensive stock risk management strategy and trading plan allows us to have a consistent source of income.

Different Types of Risk in Trading

Stock trading has two types of risk: market risk and unsystematic risk.

Market risk, also called systematic risk, is the risk that the overall market will go down, which means that all stocks will go down in value. This type of risk is beyond your control, and there's nothing you can do to avoid it. Recessions, political turbulence, interest rate changes, natural disasters, and terrorist acts are all sources of market risk. Systematic risk affects the entire market simultaneously.

On the other hand, unsystematic risk, also called specific risk, is the risk that a particular stock will go down in value, even if the overall market is doing well. This type of risk is specific to a particular company or sector and can be minimized by diversifying your portfolio.

The Securities and Exchange Commission (SEC) requires publicly traded corporations in the United States to report how their productivity and profits may be connected to the performance of financial markets. This criterion is intended to specify a company's financial risk exposure.

For example, a company that offers derivative investments or foreign exchange futures may be more vulnerable to financial risk than a company that does not provide these types of assets. This data assists investors and traders in making decisions based on their risk management policies.

How to Manage Risk

Managing your risk helps cut down losses. It can also help protect traders' and investors' accounts from losing all their money. The risk occurs when traders and investors suffer losses. However, if it can be managed, traders and investors can profit from the stock market.

Risk management is a necessary but frequently ignored prerequisite for successful, active trading.

After all, without a strong risk management technique, a trader or investor who has made big profits can lose it all with just one or two disastrous trades.

So how do you manage risks in the market?

Well, there are several ways to manage risk when trading stocks. Let's check them out:

1. Using stop-loss orders

One way to manage stock trading and investing risks is to use stop-loss orders, which automatically sell your shares if they fall below a certain price.

A stop-loss point is a price at which a trader or investor will sell a stock and incur a specified loss. This frequently occurs when a trade does not go as planned.

The points are intended to prevent the "it will come back" mentality and limit losses before they spiral out of control. For example, traders usually sell as soon as possible when a stock falls below a critical support level.

On the other hand, a take-profit point is a price at which a trader or investor will sell a stock and benefit from the trade. For example, if a stock price is approaching a crucial resistance level following a significant upward move, traders may wish to sell and take a profit before a period of consolidation occurs.

2. Using the right position size

Another way to manage risk is to use the right position size, which means only buying a certain amount of shares based on your account size.

The ratio of a single position size to total capital is called position sizing. Successful traders follow the 1% rule, which states that a position should never be more than 1% of total capital. So if you have $5,000 in the capital, the margin you designate to a position should not exceed $50.

On the other hand, professional money managers advise avoiding risking more than 2% on any single trading strategy. The excess capital protects you from a close-out by acting as a buffer against fluctuating profits and losses (P/L). Each asset has unique risk and volatility characteristics. As a result, properly altering your position sizing strategy can help you strike a balance between investment and risk.

3. Aiming for positive risk-reward ratios

Lastly, you can manage risk by aiming for the potential risk-reward ratios, which are the profit you stand to make compared to the risk you are taking.

The trading risk-reward ratio compares the potential loss to the potential return on each deal.

The risk is now defined as the price difference between your entry and stop-loss, and the reward is defined as the price difference between your entry and take profit. In essence, you just need three components to calculate the risk-reward ratio:

• Stop-loss

- Entry price

- Take profit

To calculate the risk-to-reward ratio, simply divide the potential total risk by the potential total reward:

$$\text{Risk Reward Ratio} = \text{Total Risk} \div \text{Total Reward}$$

When it comes down to planning your risk, you need to be able to answer one simple question: "How much am I willing to risk per trade?"

Answering this question helps you assess your risk tolerance, which is the very first step in developing a risk management strategy. While, ultimately, the answer to this question is a personal preference, it comes down to your risk tolerance. But, as I explained earlier, professional money managers recommend not risking more than 2% per trade.

The main advantage of the 2% risk rule is that you'll be able to take more trades at any time. Conversely, the more risk per trade you take, intuitively, you'll be prone to make fewer trades. In subsequent chapters, we will explore how to manage your risk in more detail.

So far, we have learned about risk management, its importance, types, and how we can improve our trade success and increase our profit margins by managing our risk. So just go ahead and apply what you have learned, then observe how your portfolio achieves a sustainable and profitable improvement. Meanwhile, we will look at how to find your trading edge in the next chapter.

Key Takeaways

- A risk management plan should include an evaluation of your risk tolerance and the strategies you will use to manage risk.

- There are two types of risk involved in stock trading: market risk and unsystematic risk.

- Having a risk management plan is important; your plan should include an evaluation of your risk tolerance and what strategies you will use to minimize risk.

- Some common strategies for managing risk include stop-loss orders, position sizing, and risk-reward ratios.

Chapter 8:

Finding Your Trading Edge

"Trading is not for the dabblers, the dreamers, or the desperate. It requires, above all, one steadfast trait of dedication. So if you are going to trade, trade like you mean it."
— Rod Casilli

Although there are many ways to trade the stock market, no one is perfect. The key is to find a trading strategy that fits your goals and personality.

A trading strategy is a predetermined plan for purchasing and selling securities to generate a profitable return on investment. It must be unbiased, consistent, quantitative, and verifiable.

The technique is based on fundamental or technical analyses to ensure that the unavoidable systemic risks do not have catastrophic consequences for financial instruments. When developing a trading strategy, traders should establish certain objectives.

A trading strategy can help you avoid the psychological emotions that come up during trading, but only if you follow the strategy strictly. Fortunately, this chapter covers the types of trading strategies available to beginners. It includes a discussion of the pros and cons of each strategy, as well as how to develop a trading strategy that suits your goals and personality.

Different Types of Trading Strategies

You will encounter several common trading methods when trading in the stock market. You may also discover that your success with one method is different from the success of another. It is ultimately up to you to determine which trading technique is ideal for you.

Your personality type, lifestyle, and accessible resources are all crucial elements to consider.

This section explores some of the most common trading strategies that could inspire you to get started on your stock trading journey, test a new trading strategy, or even improve your existing one.

1. Scalping

Scalping traders take very short-term trades with minor price changes.

Scalpers seek to "scalp" a modest profit from each trade, believing that the small earnings will add up.

They also often work on a risk/reward ratio of around 1:1. Scalpers typically do not make a significant profit per trade, instead concentrate on raising their overall number of smaller winning trades.

As a result, you must have a disciplined exit plan as a scalper because a large loss might wipe out many other profits accumulated slowly and methodically.

However, while scalping gives traders several trading opportunities, its biggest drawback is that it requires discipline. Scalping needs traders to be extremely disciplined because it requires higher position sizes than other trading methods. Also, you need to monitor the slightest price movements in search of profits, which can be an extremely intense activity that isn't cool for beginner traders.

2. Day trading

Day trading, also known as intraday trading, is appropriate for traders who want to actively trade during the day, typically as a full-time vocation. Day traders profit from price changes between open and closed markets.

Day traders frequently have many positions open during the day but leave them closed overnight to reduce the risk of nighttime market volatility. Day traders should stick to a well-organized plan that can quickly adjust to market fluctuations.

Generally, day trading involves limited intra-day risk, offering traders more time flexibility and multiple trade opportunities. Notwithstanding, like scalping, day trading requires discipline to make money from the stock market.

3. Swing trading

Swing trading refers to taking both sides of a stock market swing. Swing traders target a stock when they believe the market will increase. Otherwise, they can sell a stock if they think its price will fall.

Swing traders profit on the market's oscillations, which occur when the price swings from overbought to oversold. Swing trading is strictly a specialized technique for market analysis, accomplished by studying charts and understanding the individual moves that make up a larger picture trend.

Swing trading refers to taking both sides of a stock market move. Swing traders look for a stock to buy when they believe the market will climb. Otherwise, they can sell a stock if they feel it will fall in value.

Swing trading also offers many trade opportunities and can be more suitable for people with limited time compared to the trading strategies we discussed earlier. However, it does require some research to understand how oscillation patterns work. Also, some trades will be held overnight, incurring additional risks, though you can mitigate this by placing a stop-loss order on your positions.

4. **Trend following**

When traders employ technical analysis to identify a trend, they only enter trades in the direction of the predetermined trend. You have probably heard the famous trading motto: "The trend is your friend."

Well, it indeed is. The above motto is one of the most accurate in the markets. Following the trend is not the same as being "bullish" or "bearish."

Trend traders do not have a predetermined idea of where or in what direction the market should go. Trend trading success can be defined as having an accurate technique for determining and following trends. However, it is critical to be vigilant and adaptable because the trend can shift quickly.

Trend traders must know the hazards associated with market reversals, which can be lessened by using a trailing stop-loss order.

Now, it's worth noting that each of these strategies we have covered here has different risks and rewards. So it's important to choose one that fits your goals.

Basic Strategies for Traders

As a newbie in this field, you need to be more careful of your trading strategies as you start your steps in the stock market world.

In this section, we will discuss only some valuable strategies every beginner should know. These trading strategies might be a good fit if you're just starting.

1. **Buy stocks using the 52-week high/low levels**

Traders use the 52-week high/low levels as a technical indicator when analyzing a stock's current value and its future price movement.

Traders usually show an increased interest in a particular stock when its price is near the high or low end of its 52-week price range. The range generally exists between the 52-week low and the 52-week high, and these levels are based on the daily closing price of the stock.

It is worth noting that a stock may often break out to a new 52-week high intraday, a bullish signal indicating the stock is in an uptrend. However, it may also end up closing below the previous 52-week high, thus going unrecognized. This also applies when a stock makes a new 52-week low intraday but fails to close below the new 52-week low. The 52-week high/low helps traders predict whether the ongoing trend will continue or reverse.

2. Buy heavily shorted stocks

Generally, significantly shorted companies have a negative business sentiment due to industry- or company-specific causes. Investors bet on stocks that are moving lower or heavily shorted. However, markets are volatile, and the slightest good news might spark a rapid turnaround rise.

Any significant upward movement in highly shorted stocks results in a subsequent spike due to a short squeeze. Your concentration should be on heavily shorted stocks with strong fundamentals or growth prospects. The worst-case scenario is that no short squeeze rally occurs. Nonetheless, you would be comfortable holding these stocks for the medium to long-term.

3. Buy a diversified portfolio of stocks

You've probably heard the adage, "Don't put all your eggs in one basket." The idea is that if a farmer trips while bringing a basket of eggs back from the henhouse, they could wind up in a sticky predicament. Those words of wisdom transcend farming and effectively express the concept of not putting all your money into a single venture.

Diversifying their portfolio is one way investors can profit from the stock market while lowering their risk of a shattered nest egg. You could just buy a diversified portfolio of stocks and hold it long-term. Hold on to a good stock instead of selling at the first hint of profit. Keeping the stock with you could lead to more gains in the future.

One crucial rule to remember when trading stocks is the golden rule of "buy low and sell high." This means that you should look for stocks that are currently undervalued and selling at a lower price than they are worth and then sell them when their value increases.

The key is finding the trading strategy that fits your goals and personality, as these are just general ideas of the simple but effective trading strategies traders commonly use. The specifics will depend on the stock you're trading or investing in and other factors.

How to Develop a Trading Strategy

The best way to develop a trading strategy is to start with a simple system and then build on it as you gain more experience. Now, let's go through the step-by-step process:

- **Determine your trading style:** The first step in developing your stock trading strategy is determining your trading style. Determine if you are a scalper, day trader, swing trader, or trend follower; then, select a time frame—hourly, daily, weekly, monthly, and so on.

- **Determine which market condition you will concentrate on:** Trend, range, and breakout are the three primary conditions. Each of these factors has its market tone. As a result, a method that works well for trend trading may perform poorly when the market is in a range.

- **Select your tools:** Will you employ technical indicators, and if so, which ones? There are two types of strategies: indicator strategies and no-indicator strategies. Many technical indicators exist to help you identify market movement if you prefer an indicator technique. Candlestick patterns, chart patterns, trendlines, other price action features, and news trading can all be used in no-indicator techniques.

- **Define your strategy's setup (necessary circumstances) and trigger (entry rule):** The setup could be a positive market circumstance, which is important but insufficient to open the trade. It could also refer to a certain placement of candlesticks or indicators on a technical chart (more on technical analysis in subsequent chapters). The setup indicates a good time to trade but does not specify when you should enter it.

- **Set rigorous risk management measures:** These include risk/reward ratio and position size. The most typical ratio between possible loss and profit is one to three.

- **Create an exit rule for Take Profit and Stop-Loss orders:** There is not just an entry trigger but also an exit trigger. An exit trigger is the point at which you recognize it is time to call it quits on your business. The exit trigger is essential when you lose because the market won't always be in your favor.

- **Make a list of your strategy's rules:** Even if you are confident that you remember every stage of your plan, it is critical to write them down so that you do not hesitate when it is time to trade.

- **Use a sample account to test your strategy:** Make a good effort; this will lay the groundwork for your success. If there are any errors, you can fix them without losing money. It is best to look at historical data and charts surrounding the time range to be traded to see how an asset performed in the past. Make a list of your ideas and then begin backtesting them until you see some promising outcomes.

- **Go live:** Finally, begin implementing your technique on live accounts. Don't deviate from your guidelines, but keep learning and thinking about improving your method.

Meanwhile, backtesting means testing your strategy on historical data to see how it would have performed. You need to be sure to paper trade your system, which means trading it with fake money to see how it works in real life. You want to be entirely sure that your strategy works before using it on real money. This will incorporate your personal preferences, such as risk tolerance, and the kinds of industries and companies you want to trade.

Once you can define your trading strategy, we will focus on the step-by-step process for picking stocks. Picking a good stock requires you to research and look at company reports before investing money into its shares or derivatives. It is also necessary to understand how the stock market in your country works before making any investment decisions. We will go into more detail about picking stocks in the next chapter.

Key Takeaways

- There are many trading strategies, each with its advantages and disadvantages. However, it is ultimately up to you to determine the ideal one for you.

- Finding a trading strategy that fits your goals and personality is important.

- Some starter strategies for traders include buying stocks that are breaking out to new 52-week highs and those that are being heavily shorted.

Chapter 9:

How to Pick Stocks If You Like Burning Money

"Only buy something that you'd be perfectly happy to hold if the market shut down for 10 years."
— Warren Buffett

So you have finally decided to start trading and investing in stocks. But hold on! With tens of thousands of stocks to choose from, how can you pick a few worth purchasing?

Well, there are a lot of ways to pick a stock. But guess what? There's no single "right way" to pick stocks! That's right.

However, many strategies exist which are completely wrong and will lead you astray. Of course, nobody's perfect. We will all have our ups and downs, especially regarding investing. However, some mistakes you may make while selecting stocks are widespread and not limited to you alone. In truth, most investors commit many of the following errors.

The good news is that you can avoid most of these errors just by being attentive. So in this chapter, we will look at a list of mistakes rookie traders make when picking stocks that lead them to lose money. We will also discuss ways in which you may be able to avoid them—or even turn them to your advantage.

Picking Stocks Based On Price

One common mistake beginner traders make is to chase after hot stocks that have gone up a lot in price. But this is often a recipe for disaster, as these stocks are often due for a correction. For example, some stocks may surge or even double in value one year, but for one reason or another, that success may not reflect the year after.

Another mistake rookies make is to pick stocks simply because they're cheap. A good example of such stocks is penny stocks which trade for less than $5 per share; in fact, many are priced well below $1. Beginners may find the ability to purchase thousands of shares for a few hundred dollars (or less) intriguing. However, that's a problem because penny stocks are frequently associated with unproven, unsuccessful, and sometimes unethical businesses. They're also usually volatile and readily used by con artists to scam people.

Scammers buy stock, then promote it on the media and the internet so that others buy in and push up the price. Afterward, they sell their shares, causing the price to plummet and leaving other investors to suffer losses. It's known as a "pump-and-dump" scheme.

A company priced at $2 per share is not necessarily a steal, and it is more likely to collapse to $0.50 or $0.10 per share rather than double or triple in value. Meanwhile, a $200 stock can be a bargain, doubling or tripling within a few years. So you just need to evaluate the company's financials before buying.

Picking Stocks Based on a "Hot Tip"

Another mistake is to pick stocks based on a hot tip from a friend or family member. Many beginning investors place too much trust in financial TV talking heads or hot stock advice from friends or coworkers.

Just because someone you know made money on a stock doesn't mean it's a good investment. Chances are, unless the person you're speaking with is a professional trader, they're not exactly the most credible source of trading advice.

Anyone can recommend a stock, but you rarely know the person's track record. Besides, even the best investors make mistakes.

Cold callers who interrupt an evening with an urgent pitch to put money into a one-of-a-kind, can't-lose investment, such as a company allegedly on the verge of curing a disease or hitting gold or oil, can also defraud investors. Remember, if it sounds too good to be true, it probably is.

Picking Stocks Based on Emotions

Too many rookie (and seasoned) investors will acquire shares of firms based on excitement, FOMO (fear of missing out), or even greed, with minimal consideration given to whether the stocks are undervalued or overvalued. This is dangerous because overvalued stocks are more likely to experience significant losses than undervalued stocks.

Many investors will also sell in a panic if the market as a whole or one or more of their equities fall. It's vital to remember that stock values fluctuate and that investing requires a long-term perspective. So, expect the market to be volatile, and prepare yourself for a downturn every few years, knowing that the market has always recovered after a downturn. This is why you should not invest money you will need in a few years. You are more likely to make poor trading judgments if you allow your emotions to guide you.

Determine the cause of a stock's decline if it occurs. Then, consider holding on if the reason is temporary, such as a fire outbreak at a manufacturing site or high raw material prices. However, consider selling if the company faces long-term issues, such as a new, formidable competitor, a major accounting scandal, or harsh regulations. Keep emotions out of your investing and try to be as reasonable as possible.

Not Having a Plan Beforehand

Another common mistake is not having a plan before entering a trade. To prevent becoming a pawn to your emotions, you must have a plan ahead of time.

You want to develop a personal strategy that considers your risk and investment preferences. For example, are you seeking stocks with a large profit potential or dividend yield?

You also want to know your entry and exit points and where to place your stop-loss. Not having a plan is a recipe for disaster, as you will be more likely to make impulsive decisions.

Blindly Following Someone Else's Strategy

Inexperienced investors tend to follow any advice made by ostensible stock exchange pros while purchasing shares. They fail to realize, however, that once the next great thing is already in the press, it is no longer an insider tip. The stock may have achieved its top by the time the media becomes involved. At that moment, the investment is almost certainly overpriced.

Television, newspapers, and the internet (including social media) can all push equities to overly high valuations. This means that alleged insider information should be handled with extreme caution and not be used to justify failing to undertake one's risk assessment for the stock.

Just because a certain strategy worked for someone else doesn't mean it will work for you. You need to find a strategy that fits your own goals and personality. Don't blindly follow someone else's lead, as you will likely lose money.

Not Diversifying

Putting all your money into one stock is risky because a single unfavorable event could devastate your entire portfolio and, as a result, your financial future.

Diversifying your portfolio reduces this risk by ensuring that if one of your investments underperforms, it may not impact your entire portfolio.

You can diversify across various industries, such as investing a portion in technology, automobile, manufacturing, etc. If the automobile industry is performing poorly, the technology industry might perform well, helping you reduce your losses.

Investing in various companies within the same industry is another strategy to diversify.

You can also acquire many sector funds, each focusing on a different area, such as technology or finance.

Choosing Companies Simply Because They're Popular

Another mistake occurs when investors flock to the current "hottest" industry or firm but know little about it. However, just because a firm is well known or you appreciate its products does not imply that it is a wise investment. You risk losing your hard-earned money if you don't conduct adequate research, especially if you don't know the company's financial soundness. When you investigate and understand a company and its industry, you have a natural advantage over most other investors.

However, when you invest outside your knowledge set, you may be unfamiliar with the nuances and complexities of the company you're interested in. This is not to suggest that you must be a civil engineer to invest in the construction industry or a medical practitioner to invest in healthcare companies. Still, proper due diligence is critical, or consider hiring a financial advisor to help. Either way, you need to research and ensure the company is financially sound before investing.

Not Doing Enough Research

Not performing due diligence when investing can be a costly mistake. So, don't get caught up in the pretty picture that a company paints of itself. Just because a company looks good on the surface doesn't mean it is.

Always perform proper due diligence as an investor, especially with highly speculative and volatile penny stock shares. Make sure to do your research and read financial statements before investing. Typically, the more due diligence you do, the better your investing results. You're much less likely to be shocked by an event if you've reviewed everything about the company, including any warning signs and potential risks.

Focusing on the Short-Term

According to a study conducted by economics professors Andreas Hackethal and Steffen Meyer for the magazine Finanztest, private investors missed out on large stock market returns between 2005 and 2015.

The research looked at the stock portfolios of 40,000 direct bank customers. These investors earned an average return of 3.1%, considerably below the market's yearly growth rate of 8.7%. This was due to short-term trading and rash decisions rather than a lack of stock market understanding.

Private investors frequently lack the calmness to hold on to their firm stocks even when the share price is decreasing. At the same time, they tend to sell too soon when the share price is rising.

In both cases, they miss valuable opportunities. Even though prices seem volatile in the short-term, you need to look at how the price moves in longer time frames to confirm the trend. If you focus too much on the short-term, you will likely make impulsive decisions that are not based on sound analysis.

Not Having an Exit Plan

You must have an exit strategy in place to ensure that you stick to the decisions indicated in your trading plan. Having an entry plan is just as important as having an exit plan. You need to know when to sell a stock and have a stop-loss in place if the stock price goes down.

Without a plan, you're more likely to make decisions based on emotions, such as fear and greed, which may cause you to take profits too soon or run your losses too long. If you don't have an exit plan, you will likely hold on to a losing position for too long.

You'll be able to limit your risks and increase your chances of locking in earnings if you know when you're going to leave.

Meanwhile, you shouldn't forget to consider your risk-reward ratio (RRR) when planning your exit strategy.

Ideally, you won't commit too many of these common mistakes. Yet, many stock traders and investors still make some of them. Luckily, you can learn from these mistakes and phase them out quickly enough. That way, you can be in a better and more profitable situation and still have funds remaining to invest, especially as we head into the next chapter, where we will go over fundamental analysis.

Key Takeaways

- Don't pick stocks based on price, a hot tip, or emotion.

- Have a plan before entering a trade, and make sure to diversify.

- Do your research and focus on the long-term trend when investing.

- Don't chase the next big thing blindly; just because a certain strategy worked for someone else doesn't mean it will work for you.

Chapter 10:

Fundamentals First

"The fundamental law of investing is the uncertainty of the future."
— Peter Bernstein

When considering trading or investing in a stock, do you ever check the company's products, financial statements, management team, or markets in which the company operates?

Well, that's what fundamental analysis is all about!

Many people who decide to try trading are mesmerized by flashing stock charts and line graphs. But you must first nail the fundamentals if you want to earn sizable investment returns.

With fundamental analysis, you can acquire as much information as possible to understand a firm better and determine its stock's intrinsic or actual worth. Thus, it's an effective strategy for determining which firm (or companies) to invest in.

This chapter covers the different types of fundamental analysis available to beginners. It also includes a discussion of each strategy's pros and cons and how to develop a fundamental analysis strategy that suits your goals and personality.

What Is Fundamental Analysis?

Fundamental analysis involves understanding a firm and some aspects that may influence its stock price. It can help you grasp a company's true value, which can help you decide if it's the perfect investment for your portfolio. In essence, fundamental analysis involves measuring a stock's intrinsic value.

There are a few ways to conduct financial analysis, but the most common is reviewing a company's financial statements. These include its balance sheet, income statement, and cash flow statement. By reviewing these statements, you can better understand a company's profitability, debt levels, and cash flow.

And when it comes to using fundamentals analysis to find a stock to trade or invest in, there are several ways to do this. One way is to find undervalued stocks, which means looking for companies trading for less than their intrinsic value. Another way to use fundamental analysis is to find companies with strong fundamentals—in other words, companies with strong financials that are in good shape overall.

Types of Fundamental Analysis

There are two types of fundamental analysis: qualitative and quantitative fundamental analysis. Now, let's take a close look at them.

Qualitative fundamental analysis is the evaluation of a company's overall health. Below are the factors you want to consider when doing this type of analysis:

- **Industry:** What industry does the company belong to, and what is the overall health of that industry?

- **Management:** What is the quality of the company's management? Do they have a good track record?

- **Competitive advantages:** Does the company have any competitive advantages?

- **Growth potential:** Is the company in a growth industry?

Meanwhile, fundamental quantitative analysis involves reviewing a company's financial statements. You want to focus on the numbers and figures of the company with this type of analysis. Therefore, the following are the things you want to look at when doing quantitative analysis:

- **Profitability:** How profitable is the company? What is the trend in profitability?

- **Debt levels:** How much debt does the company have?

- **Cash flow:** Does the company have positive cash flow?

Let's get into more detail on how to perform a fundamental analysis of a company before buying its stocks.

A Step-by-Step Guide to Fundamental Analysis

As you can see, fundamental analysis examines ongoing industry trends, economic outlook, competitor companies' performance, and financial data. To get you on track, here's a step-by-step process you can use to perform fundamental analysis on a stock:

- **Pick a company:** The first step is to pick a company you want to analyze. Ideally, you want to pick a company in an industry you're familiar with and have access to its financial statements. You can use sites such as Yahoo Finance and Google Finance to look up publicly traded companies.

- **Review the balance sheet:** This is where the quantitative portion of the analysis happens. The balance sheet records the company's assets, liabilities, and equity at a given time. You should also check the company's debt levels; for example, Coca-Cola has more debt than equity but earns higher returns on assets than the rest of the industry.

- **Assess the income statement:** The income statement assesses a company's performance over a set period. This is where you check the company's profitability, its profitability trend over time, and expenses from the business operations for that period.

- **Evaluate the cash flow statement:** The cash flow statement represents a record of how much cash is coming in and out of the company over a period. So you want to use this report to check if the company has a positive cash flow, as it's a more conservative way to measure its performance.

- **Do your research:** In addition to reviewing the financial statements, you should also research the company. This includes reading news articles and analyst reports, and the qualitative factors of fundamental analysis that come into play.

- **Valuation:** Once you've gathered all the information, you can evaluate the stock. There are a few different ways to do this, but one of the most common is using a discounted cash flow model, which you will learn about in the next section.

- **Decision:** After your analysis, you should have a good idea of whether or not the stock is a good investment. If you think the stock is undervalued, you may want to consider buying it. However, if you think the stock is overvalued, you may want to short or sell it if you are already have the stock.

Discounted Cash Flow Model

Discounted cash flow (DCF) is a valuation method used to estimate a company's or project's value by discounting its future cash flows to present value. For some people, discounted cash flow (DCF) valuation seems like a financial art form, best left to finance PhDs and Wall Street technical wizards. DCF intricacies do involve complex math and financial modeling.

Yet, if you understand the basic concepts behind DCF, you can perform back-of-the-envelope calculations to help you make investment decisions or value small businesses. DCF analyses use future free cash flows and discount them, using a required rate of return, to arrive at the present value. The discount rate you use is important because it will affect the final value of the stock.

There are two methods for calculating DCF: the income approach and the asset approach.

The income approach discounts a company's future cash flows to present value, while the asset approach discounts the sum of a company's future cash inflows and outflows to present value. The income approach is the more common method used in DCF analysis. The asset approach is less common because it is more difficult to estimate future cash flows.

Now, when calculating the value of a stock using the DCF model, the math involved isn't exactly simple. Fortunately, some good DCF valuation calculators will handle the hard work for you, but understanding how the approach works is still crucial. Here's the formula for calculating DCF:

The huge E symbol at the beginning of the formula is the Greek letter sigma, representing the sum of multiple quantities. In other words, this symbol instructs you to compute the present value of each year's cash flow and then add them all.

The "r" in the formula represents the discount rate, while the "year" represents the years in the future.

The discount rate is a required rate of return—that is, the minimum return an investor requires to invest in a project or company. It is also known as the discount rate. A simple way to find the rate of return on a given stock is to calculate the ROI for the stock in the past several years. So you would take the annual return for each year and divide it by the purchase price. For example, if a stock returned 10% last year and you purchased it at $100, your ROI would be 10%.

In addition, we've got the free cash flows, which are the cash a company has available for distribution to its shareholders after paying all of its expenses. Free cash flows can be used to reinvest in the business, pay dividends, or repurchase shares. A company's free cash flows can be found on its balance sheet and income statement. Free cash flow is calculated as operating cash flow minus capital expenditures.

Operating cash flow is the cash that a company generates from its normal business operations. Capital expenditures are funds a company spends on long-term assets or investments, such as new factory equipment or real estate.

Finally, remember that you don't have to calculate the value of every stock you come across—only those that you're keenly interested in investing in and want to be doubly sure that the numbers make sense.

Now that we've covered fundamental analysis, we'll talk about technical analysis in the next chapter, as it's the second school of thought in the capital market with which traders and investors make their decisions.

Key Takeaways

- The key to successful stock market investing is in having a process and framework you can follow.

- Beginners should look for stocks that have positive cash flow and trends in cash flow.

- The discount rate you use is important because it will affect the final value of the stock.

Chapter 11:
Technical Analysis

"I just wait until there is money lying in the corner, and all I have to do is go over there and pick it up. I do nothing in the meantime."
— Jim Rogers

For traders who aren't comfortable leaving the fate of their investments up to chance and speculation, technical analysis is the antidote to gambling your money away. Unlike fundamental analysis, technical analysis doesn't deal with actual fundamental data but with market data like historical prices.

This chapter covers the different types of technical analysis available to beginners. It also discusses each strategy's pros and cons and how to develop a technical analysis strategy that suits your goals and personality.

What Is Technical Analysis?

Technical analysis is the process of evaluating security to determine its future price movements. As a technical analyst, you believe by analyzing past price data, you can identify patterns that will help you predict possible future price movements.

Technical analysis is based only on stock price or volume information. The goal is not to forecast the future but to identify the most plausible situations. Price action is used to predict how market participants will act based on how they have performed in the past.

Technical analysts discover trading opportunities with a high probability of success by analyzing chart patterns and trends, support and resistance levels, and price and volume behavior.

While fundamental analysis focuses on long-term factors affecting a security's price over months or years, technical analysis focuses on short-term price movements. Therefore, technical analysis suits traders looking to leverage short-term opportunities better.

The primary difference between fundamental and technical analysis is the time frame each focuses on. Also, technical analysis does not consider the underlying business or the economics that affect the value of a company.

Now, you might be wondering which one is better. Well, there is no definitive answer as to which approach is better. Successful investors use fundamental and technical analysis to make more informed investment decisions.

It is important to remember that no single method is guaranteed to be successful and that it is often helpful to use multiple approaches to get a well-rounded view before making an investment decision.

Technical Analysis Tools

This section will look at the many technical analysis tools available to you and how to use them in the stock market.

- **Charts:** The first step to becoming a technical analyst is choosing which chart type to use for technical analysis. Chart types include line, bar, and candlestick. But the candlestick chart is the most popular type for stock technical analysis.

- **Support and resistance levels:** These are two terms that technical analyzers frequently use. These are the phrases used to describe pricing levels. A support level denotes a stock's low level, whereas a resistance level suggests that the stock's price is rising. Support signals a trader to purchase a stock, while resistance signals a trader to sell.

- **Trend lines:** These are diagonal lines drawn on the chart to determine the support and resistance levels.

- **Momentum oscillators:** These are indicators that measure from zero to 100. Momentum oscillators are used to determine the movement and strength of a stock. That way, you could predict when to buy or sell a stock.

- **Moving averages:** The closing price of a stock is plotted on a chart using the moving average indicator for a specified period of all those prices. For instance, day traders use moving averages of 150 and 200 to determine the average price of a stock for the past 150 and 200 days, respectively. That way, they can decide whether to buy or sell.

In the next couple of chapters, we'll look at how to use indicators to identify trading opportunities.

Developing a Technical Analysis Strategy

First, you need to have a trading plan ready before developing a successful technical analysis strategy. This is important because you need to know what trading strategy is best for you and how much you are willing to risk for every trade you take.

Once you're convinced your plan is ready, the steps below will assist you in using technical analysis as part of your trading strategy.

- **Define your goals:** This is the first step in technical analysis for traders. It is where you usually decide what trading system to use, whether you want to trade following the trend or just do day trading and take your profits at the end of the day.

- **Choose your trading time frame:** Depending on whether you want to scalp, day trade, swing trade, or do trend following, you want to select the right time frame to execute your trades. For instance, scalpers use 1 and 5 mins time frames, day traders usually use fifteen- and thirty-minute time frames, while swing traders use one- and four-hour time frames.

- **Draw support and resistance levels:** Drawing the support and resistance levels will enable you to identify areas where an asset's price is likely to reverse or break out. A support level is when an asset's downward price trend slows as buying demand grows, causing the trend to reverse and turn higher. A similar logic applies to resistance levels, where the asset's upward price momentum decreases, and the price is likely to revert and fall.

- **Establish entry and exit points:** While identifying entry areas around your support and resistance levels, you also want to determine where you'll exit—perhaps, at the next support or resistance level.

- **Select the technical indicators you will use:** There are other factors you want to consider when determining your entry and exit positions. These include the values of technical indicators such as the moving average, relative strength index (RSI), and average true range (ATR). They can help you establish whether there's sufficient momentum behind a price move.

- **Position sizing and risk management:** As discussed in previous chapters, successful traders use the right position size and only risk a small percentage of the capital for every trade they take. So depending on your chosen risk/reward ratio, you want to determine where to place your stop-loss once you've identified an entry position.

- **Backtest/paper trade your strategy:** Backtesting involves assessing whether your trading strategy could perform well and would have paid off in reality. It's a valuable component when developing an effective trading strategy. Several online brokerage systems provide sophisticated paper trading capabilities via demo accounts or as a service to their existing customers. So don't hesitate to paper-test your strategy.

- **Implement your strategy:** Finally, it's time to go live and implement your strategy. And with your growing experience and knowledge, your trading strategy will improve. But let's not leave this to chance. Plan how you will monitor your results, obtain feedback, and improve your trading strategy.

- **Forward test your trading strategy:** Plan to take good notes of your market observations. Record your trades, keep your chart images in good order, and avoid drastic changes to your trading strategy. For this final step (which might take forever), remember that you aim to achieve positive expectancy with every trade, not positive profits for each trade. So let statistics work for you; don't force your will on the market.

Although this is a rough blueprint for how to include technical analysis in your trading strategy, we'll look at some specific tools and methods you can use with your trading strategy in subsequent chapters. Meanwhile, in the next chapter, we'll explore how to use candlestick patterns to find lucrative stock opportunities.

Key Takeaways

- Technical analysis is the process of evaluating security to determine its future price movements.

- There are many types of technical analysis, but some of the most common include momentum indicators, moving averages, support and resistance levels, and trend lines.

- When developing a technical analysis strategy, it is important to define your goals, choose the time frame you will trade in, select the technical indicators you will use, and backtest your strategy.

Chapter 12:
Candlestick Patterns

"Do not anticipate and move without market confirmation—being a little late in your trade is your insurance that you are right or wrong."
— Jesse Livermore

In the previous chapter, we talked about the candlestick chart and how it's the most popular type of chart that traders and even investors use to analyze the stock market.

However, the fact that candlestick charting is popular doesn't mean it's flawless. Regardless, exploring the candlestick chart in detail still makes sense so you can know which strategies work best and when to use them.

According to Steve Nison, candlestick charting first appeared after 1850. A great rice trader named Homma from the village of Sakata deserves much of the credit for candlestick development and charting. His original ideas were most likely developed and refined through many years of trading, resulting in the candlestick charting style we use today.

This chapter covers what a candlestick represents and the different candlestick patterns available to beginners. It also discusses how to develop a candlestick pattern strategy that suits your goals and personality.

Candlestick Formation

Candlestick charts are financial charts that visualize the trading activity for a particular security over a specified period. For instance, each candlestick on the daily time frame chart represents one trading day.

To make a candlestick chart, you'll need a data set with open, high, low, and close values for each period you wish to display. "The body" refers to the hollow or filled component of the candlestick. The long thin lines above and below the body represent the high and low range and are usually referred to as "wicks" and "tails," respectively.

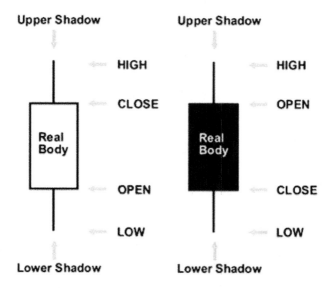

If the stock closes higher than it opened, a hollow, white, or green candlestick with the bottom of the body indicating the opening price and the top representing the closing price is drawn.

If the stock finishes lower than its opening price, a filled, black, or red candlestick is drawn with the opening price at the top and the closing price at the bottom of the body.

Candlestick patterns are formed when security price movement creates certain recognizable shapes. These patterns can predict future price movements, and traders often use them to make buying and selling decisions.

Candlestick patterns are the market's language; imagine living in a foreign nation where you don't speak the language. How can you survive if you can't even communicate? Wouldn't it be difficult?

When it comes to trading, the same thing applies. You will be able to understand what these patterns tell you about market dynamics and trader behavior if you know how to read candlestick patterns correctly. Fortunately, we will look at the different candlestick patterns throughout the remaining sections of this chapter.

Candlestick Patterns for Bull Markets

After a market decline, bullish patterns may appear, signaling a price movement reversal. They signal traders to consider taking a long position to profit from any rising trend.

1. The hammer

The hammer is a bullish candlestick pattern that forms when security prices decrease significantly after the opening but then rallies to close near the opening price.

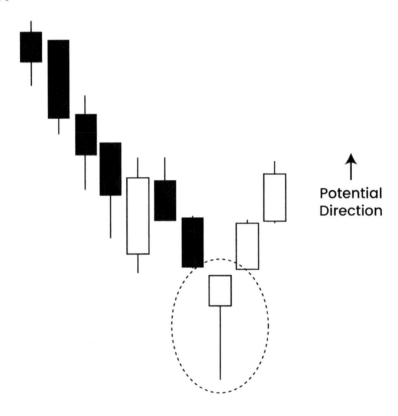

(Please note: The white candles are "Green" and the black ones "Red." This applies to every subsequent chart.)

The long lower shadow shows that the bears were in control during the session, but the bulls pushed the price back up to the opening price. This shows that there is significant buying pressure at current levels.

2. The inverted hammer

The inverted hammer is a bullish candlestick pattern that forms when the security price decreases significantly after the opening but then rallies to close above the opening price. Also, it has a long upper shadow which should be at least twice the length of the real body.

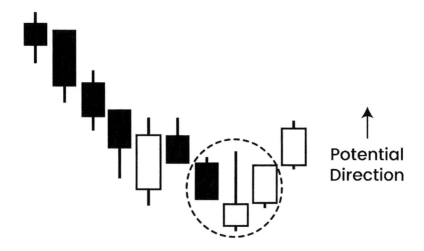

Potential Direction

The long upper shadow indicates that the bulls were in control during the session, but the bears pushed the price back down to the opening price. This shows that there is significant selling pressure at current levels.

3. **The bullish engulfing pattern**

The bullish engulfing pattern is a two-candlestick pattern that forms when a large green candlestick follows a small red candlestick.

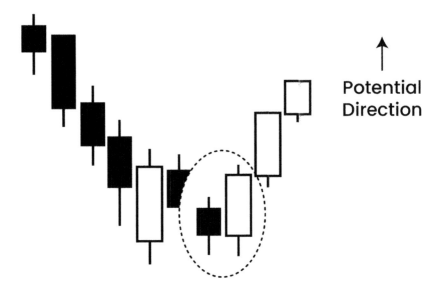

Potential
Direction

This pattern indicates that the bears were in control during the first session, but the bulls managed to take control during the second session and pushed the price higher. This shows that there is strong buying pressure at current levels.

4. The morning star

The morning star is a three-candlestick pattern that forms when a large green candlestick and another small red candlestick follow a small red candlestick.

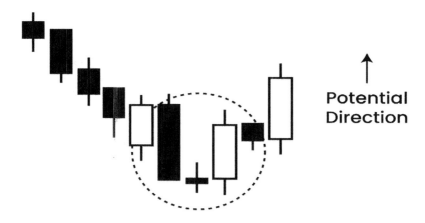

Potential
Direction

This pattern indicates that the bears were in control during the first two sessions, but the bulls managed to take control during the third session and pushed the price higher. This shows that there is strong buying pressure at current levels.

Candlestick Patterns for Bear Markets

Bearish candlestick patterns typically appear following an increase and indicate a point of resistance. When there is a lot of pessimism about the market price, traders may typically terminate their long holdings and initiate a short position to take advantage of the decreasing price.

1. **The hanging man**

The hanging man is a bearish candlestick pattern that occurs at the end of an uptrend. A small, real body forms with a long upper shadow and a small or nonexistent lower shadow.

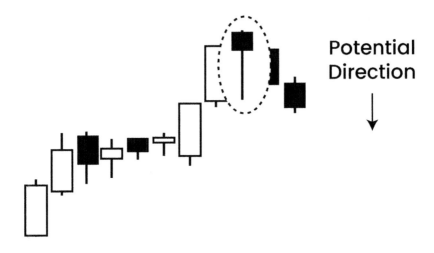

Potential Direction

The long upper shadow shows that the bulls were unable to maintain control, and the bears were able to push prices lower. This is a sign of weakness and often leads to further downside in the market.

2.   **The shooting star**

Like the hanging man, the shooting star candlestick pattern appears toward the end of an upswing. This candle is distinguished by its small body and extended upper shadow. It is the bearish counterpart to the hammer. According to professional specialists, the shadow should be twice the length of the real body.

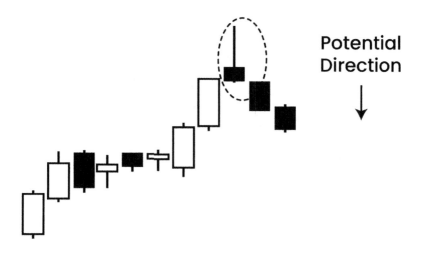

The psychology underlying the formation of this pattern is that purchasers attempted to drive the market higher but were met with selling pressure. When this candlestick forms around a level of resistance, it should be considered a high-probability setup.

3. The bearish engulfing pattern

The bearish engulfing pattern is a two-candlestick pattern that occurs at the end of an uptrend or during consolidation. It is formed by a small white/green candlestick followed by a large black/red candlestick that completely engulfs the small candlestick.

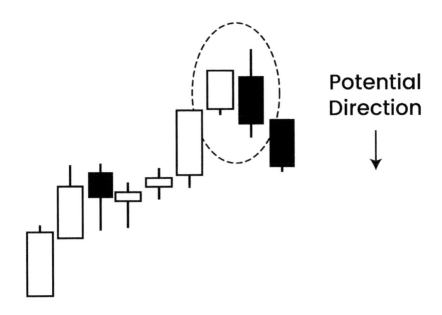

This pattern indicates that the bears are in control, and prices are likely to continue to drop.

4.   The evening star

The evening star is a three-candlestick pattern that occurs at the end of an uptrend. A large green candlestick, a small green candle, and a large red candlestick form it.

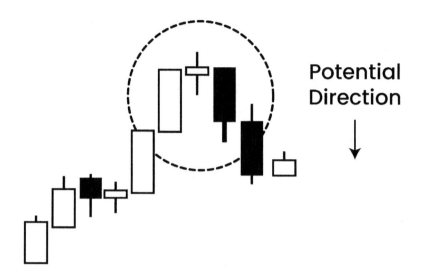

Potential Direction

This pattern indicates that the bulls are losing control and that prices are likely to continue to drop.

Candlestick Continuation Patterns

A continuation pattern occurs when a candlestick pattern does not suggest a shift in market direction. These can assist traders in identifying a period of market rest when there is market indecision or neutral price movement.

1. **The Doji**

A Doji is a candlestick that forms when the open and close are at the same price or very close to it.

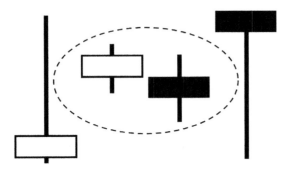

It indicates that there is indecision in the market and that prices are likely to continue in the same direction.

2.   The spinning top

The spinning top is a candlestick that can be either bullish or bearish.

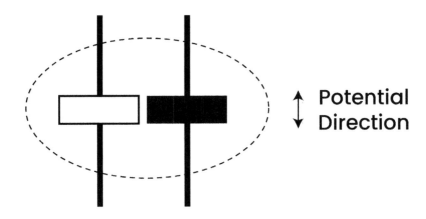

It is formed when the open and close are at the same price or very close to it, and the candlestick has a small real body. This pattern also confirms that the market is moving sideways.

3.   The falling three methods

The falling three methods are a bearish candlestick pattern that forms in an uptrend. It comprises three long black candlesticks, each close lower than the previous one.

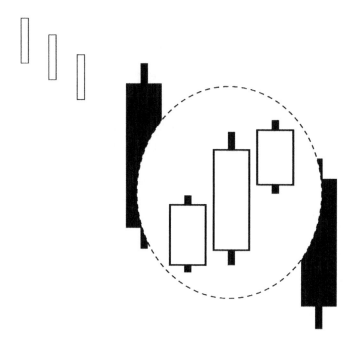

This pattern indicates that the bulls are losing control, and prices will likely continue falling.

4.   **The rising three methods**

This candlestick continuation pattern is the opposite of the falling three methods. It consists of three short reds sandwiched between two long greens.

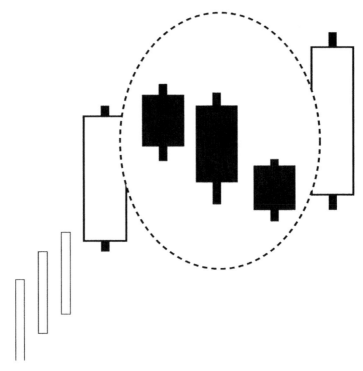

Unlike the falling three methods, this pattern indicates that the bears are losing control and that prices are likely to rise soon.

Now that you have a solid grasp of how candlesticks form and the different patterns available, it's time to advance our lessons. The next chapter will focus on key technical indicators to help you find entry points.

Key Takeaways

- Candlesticks are one way of analyzing the stock market.
- Traders can identify bullish and bearish patterns to leverage price trends.
- The morning star, hanging man, and bearish engulfing patterns are examples of candlestick patterns that traders can use to make trading decisions.

Chapter 13:

The Key Indicators to Watch

"If most traders would learn to sit on their hands 50 percent of the time, they would make a lot more money."
— Bill Lipschutz

Technical indicators are an essential component of technical analysis and are often displayed as a chart pattern to help predict market trends. Indicators typically overlay on price chart data to suggest where the price is headed or whether it is in an "overbought" or "oversold" position.

Many technical indicators have been produced, and traders are still developing new types to get better results. New indicators are frequently backtested on historical price and volume data to determine their ability to predict future events.

This chapter covers the key indicators that beginner investors should watch for, including price, volume, and open interest. We will also discuss each indicator's pros and cons and how to use them to make trading decisions. Finally, you will learn about advanced indicators and simple trading strategies to get started in the stock market.

Three Key Technical Indicators to Know

Technical indicators are mathematical calculations that predict price movements using historical price data. They are also heuristic or pattern-based signals produced by the price, volume, and open interest of a contract used by traders who follow technical analysis.

Although you can use thousands of indicators to make trading decisions, as a beginner, you only want to focus on these three key indicators:

- **Price:** The price of a stock obtained by reading candlesticks is the most important indicator because it tells you what the market is currently doing. You can use price to identify support and resistance levels, confirm trends, and identify trend reversals.

- **Volume:** Volume is the number of shares traded in a specified period. It's useful for confirming trends, identifying trend reversals, and gauging a move's strength. There are many volume indicators to choose from, including on-balance volume (OBV), Chaikin Money Flow, and the Klinger Oscillator.

- **Open interest:** Open interest is the number of outstanding contracts in a futures market. It's useful for confirming trends and identifying trend reversals. You can also use open interest to gauge the strength of a move. While there are multiple sources where you can find out the open interest of stock, the most reliable source is NSE open interest, the website of the National Stock exchange (NSE).

Advanced Indicators

As you progress in your trading journey, you may also want to use three key indicators with more subjective forms of technical analysis. Basically, that means using support and resistance levels, trend lines, moving averages, and momentum indicators to come up with trade ideas.

Although we discussed these indicators in Chapter 11, we will delve into them further in this section.

- **Support and resistance levels:** As explained earlier, these are price levels where the market tends to reverse direction. When the price rises and falls, the highest point reached before the fall becomes resistance. Resistance levels suggest areas where there will be an overabundance of sellers. When the price rises again, the lowest point hit before the decline becomes support. Support levels suggest areas where there will be an overabundance of buyers. As the price increases over time, resistance and support are constantly established. During a decline, the opposite is true. In the most basic way, you can use support and resistance levels to identify trend reversals and set stop-loss orders.

- **Trend lines:** Trend lines are technical indicators showing a trend's direction. Examples of trend lines include upward-sloping trend lines and downward-sloping trend lines. To draw trend lines properly, you want to find two major highs or lows on your chart and connect them. You can use trend lines to confirm trends and identify trend reversals.

- **Moving averages:** Moving averages are technical indicators that smooth out price data to help you confirm trends and identify trend reversals. Examples of moving averages include the simple moving average (SMA) and the exponential moving average (EMA). SMAs are the simplest form of moving averages, but they are susceptible to spikes. On the other hand, EMAs put more weight on recent prices—they place more emphasis on what traders are doing now.

- **Momentum indicators:** These are technical indicators that measure the strength of a move or trend with a scale of zero to 100. You can use momentum indicators to confirm trends and identify trend reversals. Examples of momentum indicators include the Relative Strength Index (RSI) and the stochastic oscillator. Readings of thirty or below often indicate oversold market conditions and an increase in the chance of price appreciation. In contrast, readings of seventy or more indicate overbought market conditions and an increase in the possibility of price depreciation.

- **The bid-ask spread:** The bid-ask spread is the difference between the bid and ask prices. The bid price is the price at which a stock can be purchased, and the ask price is the price at which a stock can be sold.

The bid-ask spread is the market maker's profit, and you can use it to gauge the liquidity of a stock. For instance, if the bid-ask spread is large, there are few buyers and sellers in the market, and the stock is not very liquid. But if the bid-ask spread is thin, the market is very liquid.

Simple Trading Strategies for Beginners

In Chapter 8, I shared some basic trading strategies you can use as a beginner in the stock market. This section will look at three more easy-to-follow strategies incorporating some of the techniques we have covered so far.

1. The breakout strategy

A breakout occurs when the price of a security moves past a resistance level or support level, often with increased volume, so you can use this as a signal to buy or sell a stock.

As a breakout trader, until the market breaks above the level of resistance, you will either get into a long position (purchasing a market with the idea that the asset will rise in value) or a short position (selling first and then buying later) once the market falls below the level of support.

When an asset trades over the price barrier, volatility rises, and the trader hopes the price will trend toward the breakout.

When using breakouts, monitoring an asset's support and resistance levels is critical to choosing the best instrument to trade. The more frequently an asset price hits these criteria, the more credible the breakout can be.

Next, determine your entry points. If the price is set to close above a resistance level, you will take what is known as a "bullish" or long position, seeking to profit from the rising price of the asset. If the price is set to close below a support level, you will take on a "bearish" or short position, hoping to profit from a price decline.

2. The "losing steam" strategy

The losing steam trading strategy is based on the idea that a stock's price will eventually come back down after going up. So, you would sell the stock after it rises to a certain price and "loses its steam" and buy it after it drops to its previous level.

Traders using this strategy look to closely track a price when it fails around a previous high before selling short to benefit from the price collapse.

One of the most significant advantages of using a strategy based on chart highs and lows is that risk management is relatively simple. If you want to purchase a bounce from a previous low, your stop-loss—the price at which you cancel a trade—can be set below that level. If you want to sell short as the price starts to fall, set your stop-loss above the prior high.

3. The momentum method

The momentum trading method is based on the idea that a stock's price will continue to move in the same direction if it has been moving in that direction for a while; so, you would buy the stock if it is moving up.

Trading "momentum" is considered one of the simplest trading methods for beginners. It focuses on reacting quickly to news events and recognizing large trending moves, frequently with huge volume. If the stock is trending downward, you would look to short it and buy back to make a profit.

In principle, it's easy and effective: hold your position until you see signs of a reversal, then close the trade. Don't worry if you don't understand this concept yet, as we'll get into long and short orders in subsequent chapters.

How to Use Technical Indicators

As we wrap up this chapter, it's worth noting that technical indicators are only one part of your overall trading strategy, so you don't want to go overboard with them. You should only pick the ones you're most comfortable with and that seem to work for your trading style. But then, you shouldn't rely too heavily on any one indicator; use a combination of indicators to make trading decisions. Finally, consider the fundamental factors that might affect the security price.

In the next chapter, we'll advance our lessons by exploring the different ways to place orders in the stock market. If you're trading stocks, the odds are that you'll be relying on orders as part of your overall trade strategy.

Key Takeaways

- Technical indicators are tools that traders use to make trading decisions.

- There are different types of technical indicators, and you can use them in different ways.

- It's important to remember that technical indicators are only one part of your overall trading strategy.

Chapter 14:

The Basics of Order Entry

"Stock price movements actually begin to reflect new developments before it is generally recognized that they have taken place."
— Arthur Zeikel

Trading is much more than just buying a stock. To be successful, you need to know how to place orders strategically to open up opportunities to make money.

Stock traders rely on orders to leverage price movements when they cannot personally monitor the market and protect themselves from adverse price movements.

This chapter covers the different types of orders that can be placed and how to place them. It includes a discussion of limit orders, market orders, stop orders, and how to use orders to take trading positions. It also covers the different types of brokers and how to choose a broker that suits your needs.

Placing Orders and Taking Positions

In trading, there are two types of positions: long and short.

A long position is when you buy a security with the expectation that it will go up in price, and so you make money when the price increases.

On the other hand, a short position is when you sell a security with the expectation that it will fall in price. In essence, you are agreeing to sell someone else's stocks at a certain price and make a profit by buying them back at a lower price.

A simple long position is optimistic and anticipates growth, whereas a short stock position is bearish and anticipates decline. Traders and investors use long and short positions to attain distinct outcomes. An investor may establish long and short positions simultaneously to leverage or generate revenue on security.

A long position allows the investor to earn the stock premium as income while also having the option of selling their long stock position at a guaranteed, generally higher, price. On the other hand, a short position allows the investor to buy the stock at a predetermined price while collecting the premium.

It is important to note that short positions have higher risk exposure and may be limited in IRAs and other cash accounts due to the nature of certain positions. In addition, most short positions require margin accounts, and your brokerage business must agree that more precarious positions are appropriate for you.

Typically, you need to place an order on the stock you want to trade to take a position. An order is where you state the price at which you are willing to buy or sell a security. This means you are placing an order for a particular stock at a price.

There are different types of orders, and we will look into them in the next section.

Types of Orders

Different order types can provide radically different results, so understanding their differences is crucial. Here, we'll look at the three primary order types and how they differ and when to use them: market orders, limit orders, and stop orders.

It's helpful to think of each order type as a separate tool with its function. Whether you're buying or selling, it's critical to establish your primary goal—o have your order filled swiftly at the current market price or to control the price of your trade. Then you may decide which order type is best for achieving your goal.

- **Market orders:** This is a buy or sell order for a stock at the best available price; your deal will be filled at the next available price. A market order normally guarantees execution but not the price requested. Market orders are the best option when the primary purpose is to execute the trade as soon as possible. A market order is often ideal when you believe a stock is underpriced, when you are certain you want your order filled, or when you need an immediate execution.

- **Limit orders:** This is an order to buy or sell a stock at a specified price. You can use a limit order to get the best price for your trade. But there is no guarantee that your trade will be filled at that limit price. A limit order may be useful if you believe you can buy at a lower price than the current quote or sell at a higher price than the current quote.

- **Stop orders:** A stop order is an order to buy or sell a stock when it reaches a specific price. Stop orders limit losses (stop-loss order) or lock in profits (buy-stop/take-profit order).

How to Use Orders to Take Positions

As you can see, you use orders to take stock positions. For instance, if you want to take a long position, you would place a buy order, and your trade will be filled at the next available price. However, if you want to take a short position, you will place a sell order, and your trade will be filled at the next available price.

Likewise, if you want to buy or sell a stock at a certain price below or above the current price, you will place a limit order. For example, if the stock is currently trading at $10, and you want to buy it at $9, you would place a limit order to buy at $9. However, there is no guarantee that your trade will be filled at the limit price, but if it is, you will have paid $9 per share.

Stop orders are used when you're waiting for the stock price to reach a certain point. When the price reaches that point, the stop order becomes a market order and immediately gets filled.

The difference between a limit order and a stop order is that limit orders only specify a certain price limit for how much to pay, whereas stop orders specify the exact price point at which to buy/sell a stock. Also, you generally want your limit orders to get filled, but you don't want your stop-loss orders to be triggered. That's because limit orders are used to take profit and enter positions (which you want), and stop-loss orders are used mainly to exit losing positions (which nobody likes).

The risk with using orders is that you miss filling your take-profit limit or entry orders or that your stop-loss orders are triggered at extreme price points. The catch here is that markets have a penchant for going after stop-loss orders and shying away from limit orders in the routine noise of daily fluctuations.

That makes where you place your orders a critical factor in your overall trading strategy. Ultimately, deciding where to place orders is more art than science, and even the most experienced currency traders continually grapple with where to place their orders.

In the next chapter, we'll discuss setting up a watch list to help you sort through all the stocks.

Key Takeaways

- You can place different orders, including limit orders, market orders, and stop orders.

- Orders can be used to take long or short positions in the market.

- We use stop orders to limit losses or lock in profits by specifying a particular price point to buy/sell a stock.

Chapter 15:
Building a Watch List

"I have found that when the market's going down, and you buy funds wisely, at some point in the future, you will be happy. You won't get there by reading. Now is the time to buy."
— Peter Lynch

So, now you understand trading, its specifics, and how to use fundamental and technical analysis to analyze a stock you want to trade and invest in. But then comes the question:

How do I know which stock to analyze and buy?

Answering this question when the market is reacting, like during inflation or economic recession, can be even more difficult. It's difficult to know which equities to buy in these uncertain times.

Even when picking stocks feels like swimming through a sea of red, there are lush, green possibilities. When it comes to telling which stock to trade or invest in, it all depends on what kinds of companies you're comfortable investing in; it all starts with your watch list.

This chapter covers the different types of stocks you can trade and invest in, how to build a watch list, and the types of information you should consider when building a watch list. You'll also learn about blue chip stocks, small-cap stocks, and penny stocks.

What Is a Watch List?

A watch list is a collection of stocks you are interested in but have not yet decided to buy or sell. It offers a simple way to keep track of stocks you want to buy or sell and monitor their performance over time. Also, using a watch list enables you to see real-time streaming quotes of the stocks you're interested in so you can monitor how their prices change automatically, tick by tick, with the market.

Below are the main reasons you need a watch list:

- **It helps you stay organized:** When you have a watch list, you can keep track of stocks you are interested in and the prices at which you would like to buy or sell them. This can be helpful if you are trading multiple stocks simultaneously, as keeping track of the different prices can be difficult.

- **You can monitor prices easily:** When you have a watch list, you can see how stock prices are moving and whether or not they are reaching the levels you would like to buy or sell. This can help you decide when to enter or exit trades quickly and easily.

- **You can set price alerts:** Price alerts allow you to be notified when a stock reaches a certain price, which can be helpful if you are trying to buy or sell a stock at a specific level. For example, if you are watching a stock that's currently trading at $10 per share, you could set an alert for $11 per share to notify you when the price reaches that level.

- **You can avoid emotional trading:** One of the biggest benefits of using a watch list is that it can help you to avoid emotional trading. When you trade stocks emotionally, you are more likely to make impulsive decisions that are not based on logic or reason. This can often lead to losses in your portfolio. However, if you have a watch list, you can stick to your buying and selling plans and avoid making emotional trades.

The Major Types of Stocks Every Trader Should Know

You can create a watch list based on the type of stock you want to buy and sell. For example, if you are a day or swing trader, you can create one list to track common stocks.

Similarly, you can create a list with growth and value stocks if you're following the market trend or looking to build your portfolio in the long-term.

I have shared the major stock types you should know below:

- **Common stock:** This is the most basic type of stock and represents ownership in a company. When you purchase shares of common stock, you have the right to a portion of the company's profits and a vote on certain corporate matters.

- **Preferred stock:** This type of stock typically pays higher dividends than common stock and has priority over common stock in the event of a liquidation. However, preferred shareholders often lack voting rights.

- **Convertible stock:** This type of stock can be converted into another type of security, such as bonds or preferred shares. Convertible stock allows investors to cash out their investment anytime without waiting for the company to issue new shares.

- **Callable stock:** This is a type of stock that the issuing company can redeem at a predetermined price. Callable stocks are typically issued by companies with high levels of debt, as they provide a way for the companies to reduce their debt burden.

- **Penny stocks:** These are low-priced shares of small companies that trade on over-the-counter exchanges. Penny stocks are considered to be highly speculative and risky investments, as they are often subject to manipulation and fraud.

- **Growth stocks:** These are shares of companies that are expected to experience above-average growth. Growth stocks tend to be more volatile than other types of stocks, but they also offer the potential for higher returns.

- **Value stocks:** These are shares of companies trading at a discount to their intrinsic value. Value investors believe these stocks will eventually be recognized for their true worth and traded at higher prices.

- **Income stocks:** These are shares of companies that pay regular dividends. Income investors seek a steady income from their investments rather than growth.

- **IPO stocks:** IPO (Initial Public Offering) stocks are shares of companies going public. They can be volatile, but they also offer the potential for high returns.

Your watch list is an excellent tool that can help simplify your trading and investment practices. It helps condense the activity in the stock market into a small and easy-to-see dashboard. It also enables you to identify new trends and minimize risk.

Building a Watch List

Creating a watch list is relatively easy, especially now that several platforms offer the service for free. Some of the key steps you should follow are:

- First, figure out what you're looking for by scanning the market and seeing benchmarks across industries and sectors. This will give you an idea of the specific criteria you want to set when filtering down all the stocks.

- Next, you want to decide which criteria and metrics are most important to you; this is where your trading and investing strategy will come into play.

- From here, you may want to use a stock screener to help you search through companies to find stocks that match your criteria.

- You'll want to review each company's performance; this is where technical and fundamental analysis will help you.

- Depending on your criteria and the results of your analyses, you will have a short list of stocks you're interested in

You can use various online investor news platforms like Yahoo and Google Finance to set up a watch list with price alerts. Just be sure to continually analyze news and information that are relevant to the stocks on your watch list. You may also want to set up multiple watch lists for specific types of companies or parts of your strategy.

Criteria to Consider When Building a Watch List

There are several factors to consider when building a watch list:

- **Your interest:** You should be specific about the type of stock (growth, value, income, etc.) you want to trade to enable you to trade efficiently and get your desired result.

- **Investment time frame:** You want to pick stocks that best fit your trading style (short-term, medium-term, or long-term). For instance, if you're a scalper or day trader, you want to pick stocks with good volatility and momentum.

- **Risk tolerance:** Like we already discussed, you expose yourself to risk whenever you open a position in the stock market. So you want to only add stocks whose risk you can comfortably tolerate—the options are high risk, moderate risk, and low risk. Penny stocks, for instance, are risky compared to other stock types.

- **Your investment goals:** These goals may include capital appreciation, income generation, etc.

- **Company details:** You want to check specific details about the company whose stock you want to buy. These include the following:

    - Its market capital size (large cap, small cap, micro-cap)

    - Its sector or industry

    - Its geographical location

    - Its financial health (check its debt levels, cash flow, etc.)

    - Its valuation (price-to-earnings ratio, price-to-book ratio, etc.)

- The exchange the stock is listed on

Now that you know what a watch list is, how to build one, and the type of stocks you can buy, it's time we finally start taking positions in the stock market. And this will be our entire focus throughout the next chapter.

Key Takeaways

- Stocks are divided into categories based on characteristics and performance potential.

- There are several factors to consider when building a watch list.

- Criteria for building a watch list may include the type of stock, investment time frame, risk tolerance, and investment goals.

Chapter 16:
Traders—Take Your Positions!

"It is the job of the market to turn the base material of our emotions into gold."
— Andrei Codrescu

You've identified a stock and placed your trade, and it's moving in your favor, but how do you ensure that you make a profit? That's where trade management comes in.

Unfortunately, many traders open their trades and then do nothing until they close. While this can affect your profit and loss, it can also mean that you aren't using your trading capital effectively.

Luckily, this chapter covers the different ways you can manage a trade. You will learn how to stop losses to protect your capital, take profits, and scale out of a position.

What Is Trade Management?

Trade management is managing a trade after you have placed it. It includes everything a trader does after a trade opens until it closes. By managing your trades, you can increase your profits while minimizing risk.

Trade management involves determining position size, setting stop-losses, taking profit targets, and scaling out of a position. We will cover all these topics in this chapter except for position sizing, to which I have dedicated Chapter 19.

1. Setting a stop-loss

Order management is a key part of trading. When you take a position, there should be only three outcomes: a small win, a small loss, and a big win. Big losses should not show up in your trading results. And this is where the use of a stop-loss comes in.

A stop-loss is an order to sell a security when it reaches a certain price. Traders use it to limit their losses when trading and also to help manage risk.

While there are various ways to calculate your stop-loss, you typically want it to be a percentage of your entry price. For example, if you buy a stock at $100 and place a stop-loss at $90, that's a 10% stop-loss. This means you're willing to lose 10% on the trade before getting out.

In addition, when a trade moves into a big profit, you want to take steps to lock in some profit while the trade is ongoing. First, watching a large profit turn into a small loss is demoralizing; secondly, small losses deplete your trading capital. Therefore, you can grow your accounts and compound your profits year after year by avoiding big losses.

You can also use trailing stops to squeeze more profits from winning trades. Trailing stops are a type of stop order that you set to trail a certain amount of your profit below the current trade price, and it moves up automatically as the stock moves higher.

2. Setting profit targets

Profit goals are the most crucial aspect of any trading strategy. Your exits determine whether you make a profit or a loss. Also, you must identify an appropriate profit target for your trade that provides a realistic profit aim while also providing a reasonable risk to reward.

A take profit is an order to sell a security when it reaches a certain price, and traders use it to take profits from a trade. Taking profits is important because they help you manage risk and maximize profits.

Choosing a profit target is an important component of your trading strategy because it needs you to plan ahead of time how much risk you are willing to take for how much possible return.

Like stop-losses, there are various ways to calculate your take profit. One common method is to use a price target—a specific price you expect the stock to reach. For example, if you buy a stock at $100 and place a take profit at $120, that's a 20% take profit. This means you expect the stock to increase by 20% before selling.

Scaling Out of a Position

Scaling out of a position is a technique that allows you to sell part of your position as the stock price rises, and you do this by setting take-profit targets at multiple levels. For example, if you buy a stock at $100 and it rises to $110, you might sell half your position. Then, if it rises to $120, you might sell another quarter of your position.

If you are wondering why traders scale out of positions, the answer comes down to one of the most fundamental trading principles you must accept if you want to succeed in this game. And it's that the market is not a game of chess that can be perfectly solved.

A high degree of randomness present can easily fool you into finding patterns within a cacophony of noise. In other words, there's no 100% optimal price to sell. You just cannot know it. Even the best trading algorithms developed by the most brilliant quants worldwide cannot know it.

Because of this, even though your trade idea might be perfectly valid, the specific price at which you exit the trade is somewhat arbitrary. And by putting arbitrary exit constraints on your trading, you can miss some great opportunities due to inflexible trading rules.

For this reason, some traders choose to leg out of their positions through several partial positions to lock in profits as the stock price increases and manage risk by reducing their exposure to the stock.

Likewise, if you've shorted stock and it falls to your target price, you might scale out of the position by selling part of it. This allows you to lock in profits as the stock price falls. So you'll agree that scaling out of positions can be a powerful trading technique you shouldn't hesitate to implement.

In the next chapter, we'll talk about how to find a broker to buy stocks and the necessary things to keep in mind during the search process.

Key Takeaways

- Trade management is managing a trade after it has been placed.
- Stop-losses and take profits are used to limit losses and lock in profits.
- Scaling out of a position is a technique that allows you to sell part of your position as the stock price rises.

Chapter 17:

The Truth About Brokers

"The market can stay irrational longer than you can stay solvent."
— John Maynard Keynes

Using a stockbroker is the most convenient way to buy and sell stocks. An online broker, for instance, allows you to buy stocks on its website in minutes after opening and financing your account.

However, choosing the right stockbroker to place your trades can be daunting, as we've got many out there. Fortunately, this chapter covers the types of brokers available and how to choose the one that best suits your needs. We'll talk about full-service brokers, discount brokers, and online brokers.

Also, you will learn about the different types of brokerage accounts available and how to choose an account that proffers solutions to all you need.

What Is a Broker?

Even if you are not in finance, you must have heard the word "broker."

But what exactly does it mean?

A broker is essentially a professional that buys and sells stocks on behalf of their clients. In popular culture, the phrase "stockbroker" can refer to various job titles, such as stock traders, investment brokers, commodities brokers, or bond brokers.

A broker can also serve as a financial advisor, advising customers on their investment portfolio and possibilities to help them achieve their financial goals. A client's financial position and goals will influence their optimal investment option. For example, a long-term investor seeking assistance with retirement planning will likely make different trades than an aggressive investor seeking a quick return.

There are different types of brokers, including full-service brokers, discount brokers, and online brokers. Let's examine each of them:

- **Full-service brokers**: Full-service brokers offer a complete suite of services, including investment advice, portfolio management, and execution of trades. These brokers typically have investment banking and research departments that offer their stock analysis, special products, and access to initial public offerings (IPOs).

  Clients can place trades by phoning their broker directly or using other online and mobile platforms. And this is why full-service brokers are best suited for investors who need comprehensive advice and assistance. Because of the diversified assortment of services offered, full-service typically charges higher fees than other brokers.

- **Discount brokers**: Discount brokers have closed the financial product and service gap with full-service brokers by offering independent research, mutual fund access, and basic banking products. They typically do not provide investment advice or portfolio management services; instead, they simply execute trades on behalf of their clients. Discount brokers are ideal for investors who prefer to make their own investment decisions, and as the name implies, they charge lower costs than full-service brokers.

- **Online brokers**: Online brokers are a type of broker that provides access to online trading platforms and are usually focused on simplicity. They do not offer many advanced features, such as desktop trading platforms, research reports, etc. While these brokers generally offer commission-free trading and easy-to-use mobile-based and web-based trading platforms, they are primarily designed for casual investors who want a simple way to buy and sell stocks from their mobile devices without the assistance of a broker. Online brokers are best suited for investors who are comfortable making their own investment decisions and typically charge lower fees than full-service or discount brokers.

As you can see, each type of broker has their strengths and weaknesses, so it's important to choose a broker that provides the services you want and best suits your needs. Also, these brokers usually offer different brokerage accounts that traders and investors can use to buy and sell securities.

The most common type is the standard brokerage account. You'll enjoy free withdrawals and greater flexibility because market circumstances change with this brokerage account. Other brokerage accounts include IRA accounts, 401(k) accounts, and 529 plans. Therefore, you want to choose a brokerage account that suits your needs.

What to Look for When Choosing a Trading Platform

First, what is a trading platform?

It's a trading software that serves stock traders with stock trading analysis and trade execution. These trading platforms provide charts and order-taking methods and serve as intermediaries between customers and brokers. Most can differ greatly and can vary in cost.

There are many trading platforms in the marketplace, but you must consider certain factors. Let's check them out:

- **Trading fees:** This is one of the first things most traders look at when choosing a trading platform. Trading fees are costs that the brokerage firm/ trading platform charges for each trade. Some firms also charge monthly or yearly fees in addition to trading fees.

- **Type of account:** Another factor to consider is the type of account being traded. For example, an IRA account has different rules than a standard brokerage account.

- **The platform's user interface:** The third factor to consider is the platform's user interface, as it should be easy to use and understand. You want a platform that lets you immediately place an order or close a trade. One-click trading and management of your positions are advantages that you must consider when picking a trading platform.

- **Customer service:** Finally, consider the brokerage firm's customer service. You want to choose a firm that puts its clients first, where you can easily communicate with its customer service whenever you encounter any issue. The brokerage firm should be available to answer any questions that you may have.

The Truth about Retail Trading Brokerage Firms

Statistics show that most day traders, on average, tend to lose money. While this often happens due to poor trading skills, so much money is lost regularly because that's how brokerages make their money—by getting retail traders to trade more often. And, sadly, most people don't have a clue about this and how it works.

Trading is often regarded as risky; it's also likened to visiting the casino because the platforms that allow non-professional traders to invest in stocks exploit people's ignorance.

In other words, retail trading brokerages will push traders to make risky bets and take a gambler's approach to trade stocks because it's in their best interests to do so. They go so far as to pay "trading educators" and other people who aren't true professional investors to show retail traders how to trade their money away. It's like a casino teaching you how to play poker the wrong way.

So you want to keep this in mind when deciding which broker you want to sign up with. If a brokerage is offering you a deal that seems too good to be true, chances are it is.

As I said in Chapter 7, risk is everywhere, including in the financial market. And that's why we'll look at advanced techniques for managing risk in your trades in the next chapter.

Key Takeaway

- Statistics show that, on average, most day traders lose money. This is because brokerages make money by encouraging retail traders to take a gambler's approach to trade stocks. Keep this in mind when choosing a broker, and beware of any offers that seem too good to be true.

Chapter 18:

Risk Management

"There were two sets of rules when it comes to money: One set of rules for the people who work for money and another set of rules for the rich who print money."
— Robert Kiyosaki

People tend to shy away from risk. But the irony is that risk is what creates opportunity. Yes, trading is risky, yet it offers a high potential reward. So the key here is to learn to manage the risk.

Most traders devote too much time and attention to the wrong elements of trading. Yes, trading methods, trade entry, and technical analysis are vital, but you must know what you're doing to make money. However, these plays are insufficient on their own. To gain profits, you must have the correct "fuel" on the fire. And risk management is the fuel crucial to your success.

This chapter covers the different types of risk involved in trading and how to manage them. We'll also talk about capital risk, position sizing, and diversification.

Managing Risk in Trading and Investing

Most people think trading is about maximizing your wins, but the reality is that trading is about minimizing your losses. Without taking risk management measures, traders might easily lose all their accrued gains due to one or two unsuccessful trades.

While small losses can be handled and worked through, large losses might wipe out your trading account and force you to start over. This is why being a good day trader and stock investor is about managing your risk appropriately to minimize losses.

Starting on the path of stock trading is akin to taking off on a long-distance flight. You would not take off unless you were certain there was enough fuel in the tank. Not just enough fuel, but enough reserve fuel to get you through any unexpected issues or detours along the road. It is never safe to assume that a flight will go smoothly from takeoff to landing because many variables are beyond the pilot's control.

Managing your risk in trading and investing will be your safety net to ensure you do not crash your trading account to zero, just as a flight without safety procedures could be a death trap. By reducing risk, you increase your chances of landing outsized returns.

So what can you do to minimize risk?

There are different ways to manage risk in trading and investing, including position sizing and diversification. Position sizing is the process of determining how many shares to buy or sell, especially compared to your portfolio's overall size. Meanwhile, diversification is a technique that can be used to manage risk by spreading investments across different asset classes.

Luckily, we've discussed diversification briefly in the previous chapters. However, we will still cover it in detail in the next section of this chapter. We will also focus on position sizing in the next chapter.

Risk Management Techniques for Trading and Investing in Stocks

Risk management is an important but frequently overlooked prerequisite for excellent trading performance. After all, without a strong risk management technique, a trader who has made significant profits might lose it all in just one or two disastrous trades. So here are the best ways to curb the risks of the market:

- **Diversify your portfolio:** In Chapter 7, I talked briefly about what diversifying entails and how you can go about it. Diversifying your holdings is one of the best ways to manage risk for your stock trading portfolio. It's a technique that requires you to spread your investment across various asset classes, such as stocks, bonds, and cash.

  By investing in diverse asset classes, you can minimize the risk of losing money if one asset class devalues. Positive performance in one portion of a portfolio is assumed to outperform negative performance in another. So if you diversify over numerous stocks, at least one of them will be able to compensate for the losses from the other.

- **Stick to your rules:** When trading stocks, it's important to have a set of rules that you always follow. These rules should include guidelines for when to buy and sell stocks and how much risk you're willing to take. By sticking to your rules, you can keep emotions out of your decision-making process and make more rational decisions. This is why you should set stop and limit orders.

- **Monitor your portfolio regularly:** Another important risk management technique is to monitor your portfolio regularly. This includes tracking your investments' performance and ensuring that your overall portfolio remains diversified. By monitoring your portfolio, you can ensure you're not taking more risk than you're comfortable with.

- **Hedging with options:** Although more of an advanced risk management strategy, hedging with options is another technique you can use to protect your portfolio from losses. Hedging with options is basically when you take a stock asset position and open another position in another asset. That way, if your primary position loses, your alternative position will profit and offset the risk of losses in your stock asset.

  For example, if you're worried that the stock market could crash, you could purchase options on the S&P 500 index. This would give you the right to sell the index at a certain price, and if the market did indeed crash, you would be able to offset some of your losses.

It doesn't matter whether you have a small or large capital in your trading account; a single trade shouldn't put too much of your trading capital at risk. But how exactly do you determine how much of your capital to risk per trade? Well, you'll learn about it in the next chapter, where we'll focus specifically on position sizing as a means of controlling risk.

Key Takeaways

- Risk management is important in trading and investing, as it can help to minimize losses.

- Diversification and sticking to rules are two key risk management techniques.

- Regular portfolio monitoring and hedging with options are also effective strategies to managing risk.

Chapter 19:

Position Sizing

"In a bull market, one can only belong or [stay] on the sidelines. Remember, not having a position is a position."
— *Richard Rhodes*

If you don't position size properly, you could lose all your money—even if your trade is a winner.

Position sizing refers to the ratio of a single position size to the total capital. As I explained in Chapter 7, successful traders adopt the 1% rule, which suggests that the size of a position should never exceed 1% of the total capital. This makes your remaining capital a buffer against your floating profits and losses (P/L) and protects you from a close-out.

Every stock asset has different risk factors and volatility levels. Thus, adjusting your position sizing strategy accordingly can establish a balance between your investment and the risk. In this chapter, we will talk extensively about position sizing in trading and how to calculate the right position sizing when placing a trade.

So, what are the steps to position sizing properly?

Establish Your Risk Tolerance

In Chapter 7, I explained to you what risk tolerance is. Establishing your risk tolerance is the first step in position sizing. This will help you determine the maximum amount of capital you are willing to lose on any given trade.

To establish risk tolerance, you must consider your financial goals and objectives. For instance, if you are trading for income, you will have a higher risk tolerance than if you are trading for capital preservation.

While I won't recommend it, if you risk up to 2% of your stock account per trade, then you can risk $200 per trade on a $10,000 account. You can also risk $500 on a $25,000 account, and so on.

So, I recommend sticking to the 1% rule because even the best traders can suffer a streak of losses. However, if you limit your risk for each transaction to 1%, even if you lose 10 trades in a row (which should be quite unusual!), you will still retain practically all of your capital and will overcome the losing streak in time. You'd be bankrupt if you bet 10% of your account on each deal and lost 10 in a row. Also, even if you only risk 1% (or less) on each trade, you can still make a lot of money.

Furthermore, merely risking 1% helps avoid the disaster in which you wind up losing far more than expected. A stop-loss order does not ensure an exit at the specified price. You could lose much more than 1% in an abrupt move or overnight price gap (also called slippage). If you only risk 1%, most dramatic moves result in a little percentage reduction in equity that is easily recovered. However, if you had risked 10% on the deal, such a move may have wiped out half or virtually all of your wealth.

Determine Your Entry and Exit Points

Once you establish your risk tolerance, you need to determine your entry and exit points to determine your position size. These are the prices at which you will buy and sell the stock.

It is important to have realistic expectations when setting these points, as you may miss out on potential profits if your entry point is too high or incur losses if your exit point is too low.

Set a Stop-Loss Order

You must also select a stop-loss level when determining your position size. A stop-loss order terminates a trade if the price swings against you and reaches a certain price. This order is set at a logical point outside the normal range of market movements, and if it is met, it indicates that you were wrong about the market's direction (at least for the moment).

As I have explained in the previous chapters, a stop-loss order is an order placed with a broker to sell a security when it reaches a certain price; this price is typically below the current market price. We usually use stop-loss orders to limit losses in a security position.

So let's say you buy a stock, and the price moves higher into a former resistance area but then starts moving sideways before dropping. This triggers a short trade (a method I mentioned in Chapter 2). The entry price of the short is $182, and you place a stop-loss at $200. This results in a trade risk of around

$20. Ultimately, knowing how to set your stop-loss will help determine the proper position size.

Consider Your Time Frame

When position sizing, you also need to consider your time frame, which is the length of time that you expect to hold the security. For instance, if you are a day trader, your time frame and stop-loss levels will be much shorter than if you are a long-term investor. Your trading time frame can impact the number of shares you buy or sell.

Aside from the specific trading method you employ to explore and trade the markets, where you place your stop-loss is possibly the most critical aspect of any trade you execute.

It amazes me how many people still assume that because they have a tiny account and a broad stop will cost them too much to trade, they must use tighter stop-losses. This assumption stems from the (mis)perception that a tighter stop-loss decreases a trader's risk or (equally incorrectly) increases their chances of generating money because they can increase their position size.

That's a wrong idea! The money you risk on any given trade increases or decreases when you adjust your position size. And so, if you're using wider time frames, which reduces stress and improves your lifestyle, you have to use wider stop-losses, as they enable you to set and forget trades until they hit your set profit targets. In contrast, trades with a smaller time frame will have a smaller stop-loss level, giving a small target level.

Determine the Proper Position Size

You now have all the information you need to calculate the proper position size for any trade. You know your account risk and trade risk. Since trade risk will fluctuate on each trade, and your account risk will also fluctuate over time as your balance changes, your position sizes will usually differ from one trade to the next.

To calculate position size, use the following formula for the respective market:

Let's say you have a $10,000 account, which means you can risk $100 per trade (1%). So, you buy a stock at $200 and place a stop-loss at $196, making your trade risk $4.

Stocks: $100 / $4 = 25 shares.

Twenty-five shares are your ideal position size for this trade because you are risking exactly 1% of your account based on your entry and stop-loss. The trade costs you 25 shares x $100 = $2,500. You have enough money in the account to make this trade, so leverage is not required.

You can also use a position sizing calculator to determine the appropriate number of shares to buy or sell based on your risk tolerance and other factors. There are many position-sizing calculators online, so feel free to check them out and choose the one you like.

There you have it—the five-step process to determine your position size. Finally, it is important to review your position size regularly. Doing so will ensure that it remains appropriate for your risk tolerance and other factors.

The next chapter discusses the importance of adopting a long-term perspective to trading and investing in stocks.

Key Takeaways

- You need to consider your risk tolerance, entry and exit points, time frame, and other factors when position sizing.

- Several online position-sizing calculators can help you determine the appropriate number of shares to buy or sell.

- It is important to review your position size regularly.

"Invest for the long haul. Don't get too greedy, and don't get too scared."
— Shelby M. C. Davis

Trading with enough money can make you rich in the short-term. But if you want to stay rich for the foreseeable future, you'll have to play the long game.

Although the stock market has experienced several major downturns since 2000, history shows that stock markets eventually recover—though past performance cannot guarantee future results. The chart below demonstrates how the market has fluctuated over the past decades. While stocks saw some drastic dips, they also rallied periodically for strong gains.

As of December 31, 2021

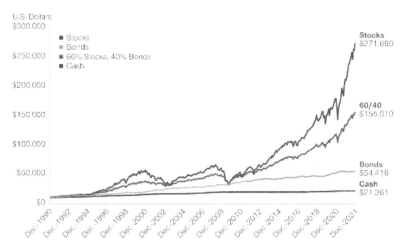

Over a long-term time horizon, stocks provide a higher return potential when compared with bonds or cash. The purple line represents a 60/40 allocation of stocks and bonds, which has generated significantly higher returns than an all-bond portfolio with less volatility than an all-stock portfolio.

Day trading and swing trading may focus on short-term positions and trades. But if your goal is to create a stable income source for yourself, then you will need a sustainable approach to trading stocks; taking a long-term view is one way to achieve this goal.

This is why we need to look at the different types of long-term strategies available as we wrap up this book. This chapter reveals strategies like value investing, growth investing, and how you can buy and hold long-term.

What Is the Long-Term View?

The long-term view is an investment strategy that considers the current market conditions and your personal financial goals. It allows you to take a more holistic approach to trading stocks and can help you weather the market's ups and downs.

There are several reasons why you might want to take a long-term view of the market:

- First, it can help you avoid making impulsive decisions based on emotions. As the chart on the previous page illustrates, short-term volatility can be violent. Knee-jerk reactions to market fluctuations can lead to buying high and selling low, making it difficult to stay on track.

- Second, it can help you focus on your financial goals. Adhering to a lengthy time horizon may not always be easy, especially in a downturn, but it can be a valuable discipline to help you achieve long-term financial goals.

- Third, it can give you a complete picture of the market. Market highs and lows have historically evened out over the long-term, as you can see at the start of this chapter.

How to Invest for the Long-Term

If you're considering paying for goals several years away, you should be more concerned about playing the long-term game. Let's check out the key ways to help pursue your long-term investing goals in the stock market.

1. Create a diversified portfolio

The concept of portfolio diversification cannot be overemphasized. It also plays a key role in investing in the long-term. This means you should not put all your eggs in one basket. Instead, you want to spread your investment across different asset classes, such as stocks, bonds, and real estate.

You should also diversify within each asset class. For example, you should not invest all your money in one stock. Instead, you should buy a basket of different stocks. You should also consider diversifying your trading strategies; that means you can use a combination of different parameters to ensure that your positions aren't always trending together. This will help to hedge your portfolio against market events that impact entire industries or parts of the world.

2. **Rebalance your portfolio regularly**

As your investment portfolio grows, the allocation of your assets will change. For example, investing in a stock that goes up in value will make up a larger percentage of your portfolio.

Rebalancing is selling some of your appreciated assets and buying other assets to maintain your original asset allocation. Rebalancing helps to reduce risk and keep your portfolio diversified.

3. **Choose the right investment strategy**

There are two main investment strategies that you can use: buy and hold or active investing. Buy and hold is a passive investment strategy where you simply buy and hold an asset for a long period, regardless of what the market is doing.

In contrast, active investing is a more aggressive strategy involving trading your assets actively, based on your market analysis.

Your chosen strategy depends on your goals, risk tolerance, and other factors.

4. **Prepare yourself for market volatility.**

The stock market is volatile, meaning prices can go up and down rapidly. When investing long-term, you need to be prepared for market volatility. You should not let short-term fluctuations in the market dictate your investment decisions. Instead, you should have a long-term plan and stick to it.

Also, always ensure that your short-term trades are helping you to meet your long-term investment goals. This will keep you on track regardless of how the market is going.

Value Investing

Value investing is a long-term investment strategy that involves selecting stocks that appear to be trading for less than their intrinsic value. Warren Buffett and his right-hand man, Charlie Munger, are big supporters of this strategy.

As a value investor, you want to actively seek out value stocks in the market that you believe are undervalued. It is a popular belief that the market overreacts to both good and bad news, resulting in stock price swings unrelated to a company's long-term fundamentals. The overreaction provides an opportunity to benefit by purchasing equities at a discount on sale.

Growth Investing

Growth investing is a strategy aimed at expanding an investor's capital. Growth investors, as opposed to value investors, often invest in growth stocks—young or small companies whose earnings are predicted to rise faster than their industry sector or the broader market.

Many investors are drawn to growth investing because investing in rising companies can generate substantial profits (as long as the companies are successful). However, because such businesses are untested, they usually carry considerable risk.

And that brings us to the end of the amazing stock trading guide. In the next section, which is the concluding part of this book, we'll recap everything we've covered so far.

Key Takeaways

- The long-term view is an investment strategy that considers the current market conditions and your personal financial goals.

- You might want to take a long-term view of the market for several reasons, including avoiding impulsive decisions and staying focused on your financial goals.

- When investing for the long-term, you must create a diversified portfolio and regularly rebalance it.

CONCLUSION

"People in markets find a way of getting down to the essentials of I have, you want; you have, I want."
— Audre Lorde

Congratulations on reading this book to the end and taking action to learn about trading and the techniques to use for different market conditions.

If you check online or walk into any bookstore, you'll find a bunch of resources from so-called trading educators and financial gurus. These resources will show you in encyclopedic style various technical indicators you can use to interpret the stock market. You'll also find books on fundamental analysis and paid information about the investment trends of the year.

Although people pay to access these resources, most times, they have trouble practicing what they've learned because they don't invest using core principles. Then, rather than look for a better option, they waste more money to access more resources, sign up for some stock picks service, or try to access automated trading systems, hoping they will just earn them money without any effort. Then, they get disappointed all over again and repeat the process.

The average person fails to use a real trading and investment strategy and is always scared in the market.

I know how it is because when I started my trading and investing journey, I read lots of great books and thought I had a strategy that could make money. However, I didn't follow through with it until I reached the point where I had to. All the stock tips and techniques you might use in the market won't help you without a solid foundation to work off of. So, before understanding your behavior as a trader or investor, you need to understand what moves stock prices and how mass psychology is a factor.

Then you'll understand how to separate yourself from the crowd, focus on what matters in the financial market, and enter investments aligned with your strategy. You'll also be able to take appropriate steps to size up your risks and control them. If you do this, you'll trade and invest in the market confidently. And that's exactly my goal for writing this book: to put you on the right path.

It isn't the stock market or stock picks that make you money; rather, it's your ability and foresight as a trader and investor. So, go ahead and start with the fundamentals, then research different stocks and companies on public exchanges. You should also find time to study stock charts. And with time, you'll start to recognize patterns in how prices move.

Once you build up those abilities, you no longer will nervously interact with the stock market like everyone else. Instead, you will approach trading confidently.

Solid trading and investment principles that never change create strategic stock trading. Sure, one individual trade may not go right, and you may even get into a trading fix from time to time. But over the long haul, using the right techniques, which I have shared in this guide, is the closest thing to a sure thing you can get out of the stock market.

Meanwhile, it would mean a great deal to me if you could take some of your time to leave a review on Amazon with your feedback on the book. And if you liked it, then do tell your friends and colleagues about it.

I wish you good luck on your trading and investing journey.

Brian Hale

Printed in Great Britain
by Amazon